# Where Gambling Can Take You

♣ ♦ ♥ ♠

by Joan I. Campbell

Copyright © 2012 by Joan I. Campbell
First Edition — April 2012

Graphic illustrations by Mat Poirier

**ISBN**
978-1-77097-266-7 (Paperback)

All rights reserved.

Permission has been given to use the real names of the people interviewed unless otherwise stated.

No part of this publication may be reproduced in any form, or by any means, electronic or mechanical, including photocopying, recording, or any information browsing, storage, or retrieval system, without permission in writing from the publisher.

Published by:

FriesenPress
Suite 300 – 852 Fort Street
Victoria, BC, Canada V8W 1H8

www.friesenpress.com

Distributed to the trade by The Ingram Book Company

# Table Of Contents

Dedication ........................................................... vii

Introduction ......................................................... ix

Synopsis ............................................................. xi

Chapter 1: My First Casino Visit ..................... 1

Chapter 2: The Positive Side .......................... 13

Chapter 3:
Employment In The Gaming Industry ............ 19

Chapter 4: The Other Side ............................. 45

Chapter 5: Casino Etiquette ........................... 61

Chapter 6: Casino Antics ............................... 65

Chapter 7: The Promotions/Perks .................. 73

Chapter 8: The Adventures ............................ 77
Melbourne, Australia ..................................... 78
The London, UK Experience .......................... 83
The Laughlin, NV Experience ........................ 88
Trip To Tunica, MS ........................................ 94
Trip To Portugal ........................................... 104
Las Vegas 'Comp' .......................................... 110

Chapter 9: Slots, Pots And Jackpots .............. 117
The Wins And Losses ................................... 118
Casino Tipping ............................................. 126

Chapter 10:
Casino Tax Rebates Vs. Govt. Tax Laws ............ 131

Chapter 11: The Down Side ........................... 133

Chapter 12: Texas Hold Em Poker .................... 141

Chapter 13: How Big Is The Industry? .............. 151

Chapter 14: Gamblers Anonymous ................. 161

About The Author ........................................ 181

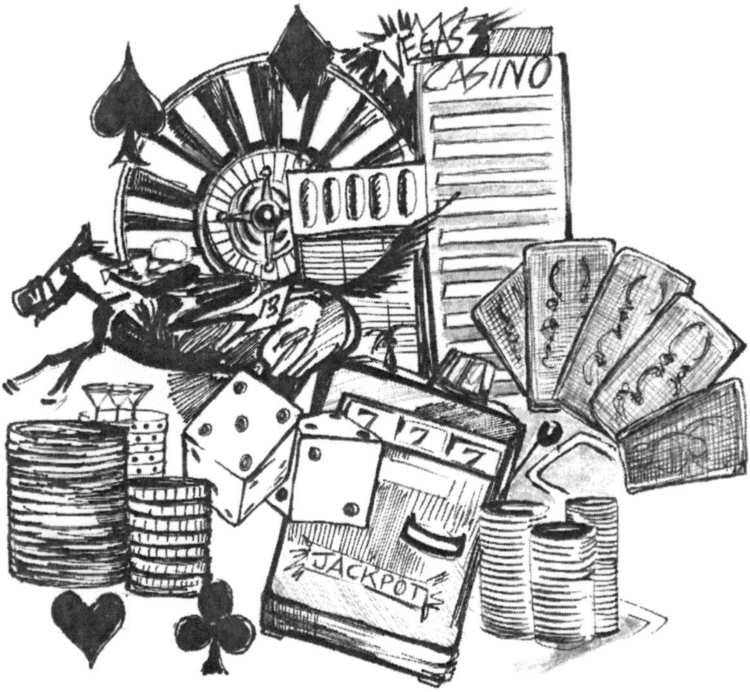
VEGAS
CASINO
13
777
JACKPOT

# DEDICATION

I dedicate this book to my wonderful family and my dear friend Marnie. Their encouragement motivated me to write this book and without their support this book probably never would have been written.

Joan C.

# INTRODUCTION

I am a retired 74-year old retired college professor, author, grandmother, wife, and gambler who enjoys meeting people and life's adventures. I have worked in retailing (part-time while attending High School in Kirkland Lake, Ontario) in business (IBM Canada in Hamilton, ON), in industry (Procter & Gamble, Hamilton), government (the Federal Government in Ottawa), and education (taught business subjects in the secondary system for the Hamilton Board of Education for 8 years, and finished my teaching career as a Business Teacher with Mohawk College A.A. & T., for 25 years). After retiring from the community college environment, I began writing for Pearson Education Canada, Higher Education Division (Pitman Office Handbook, 7e), and still do contract work with them today (presently working on the 8th edition of the Pitman Office Handbook; this 600-pg. handbook is used in Community Colleges, Business Schools, and Government).

When gambling became legal and Casinos began opening in every province in Canada as well as throughout the US and other countries, it soon became a major form of entertainment as well as one of the fastest growing employment industries in the world.

This book was not written to advocate gambling, but to show a positive side of the gaming industry and to provide in-sight into this lucrative and popular form of entertainment.

Emphasis is on Employment in the Gaming Industry, and how the casino and employees contribute to their communities. Included are interviews with casino personnel, as well as my own personal adventures at various casinos in North America and the UK.

Like any addiction, gambling, of course, can be harmful; I have labeled it "the hidden sport." Chapter 11 in the book deals with the downside stories from addicted gamblers who were kind enough to share their stories.

Let your read begin and I hope you enjoy <u>Where Gambling Can Take You</u>.

**WE ARE WHAT WE REPEATEDLY DO.**

**EXCELLENCE, THEREFORE,**

**IS NOT AN ACT BUT A HABIT.**

**Aristotle**

# SYNOPSIS

This book was written to portray the positive side of the gaming industry and how Casinos have created employment opportunities for people who have lost jobs because of the decline in the manufacturing industry and plant closures across North America. It provides a list of the many jobs within the casino environment, as well as interviews with various casino employees who enjoy employment in the gaming industry.

Casinos provide opportunities for individuals with specific job skills required for the numerous jobs that must be filled in running a casino. Information on how casinos encourage employees to take courses to enhance their knowledge, the provision of training for career advancement and how the casinos and their employees are involved in contributing to their communities is discussed as well.

My own personal adventures to casinos in Canada, Australia, the Bahamas, the United States and London, UK are shared. The adventures include interesting bits of history including my own hometown, Kirkland Lake, and the names of the many famous NHL players who hailed from there. Details of the promotions/perks, and junkets the casinos offer, as well as the wins and losses are outlined.

Tax laws in Canada and the US differ when it comes to the pay-outs for slot wins or table wins. Slot wins over US$1200 result in a 30% withholding tax, while gaming-table and slot wins in Canada are tax-free. Information is provided on how to get the withheld money back.

Gambling has become a very popular form of entertainment in the world today. I have labeled gambling 'the hidden sport' because it involves people of all ages and thousands of people are gaming but do not wish to acknowledge their participation. It can be a great venue for an outing of fun or it can turn into an addiction that is harmful and should be recognized as such. The downside and addiction stories are shared.

LEARN SOMETHING NEW EVERY DAY OR YOU HAVE LOST A DAY

♣ ♦ ♥ ♠

# CHAPTER 1
# MY FIRST CASINO VISIT

## MY FIRST CASINO VISIT

The first time I walked into a casino was when I was twenty-one years old, single and on vacation with girlfriends Carmen, and Loretta (Loretta, now deceased) for a week in Long Beach, California, and then a week in Las Vegas, Nevada. I have never forgotten the experience and still remember the excitement, the glitz and the glamour of the casinos. That excitement still prevails when I enter a casino today. We attended a few great shows on the famous strip. Frank Sinatra and the *Rat Pack were there at that time and they had a huge closing party at The Sands to celebrate the filming of the movie Oceans 11; the fountains at The Sands were sprouting pink water which looked like Pink Champagne. It truly was an evening to remember.

*In the 1960s, the Hollywood Rat Pack, as they were known, included: Dean Martin, Sammy Davis Jr., Joey Bishop, and Peter Lawford.

One evening while we were there, we had attended a floorshow at a Casino, and that is when we met the Mayor of Seal Beach, CA. We sat at a table with he and his chauffeur where we had a drink. While talking with them, we mentioned that we were going to Long Beach, CA the next week. He gave us his business card and said call him when we got to the LA Airport. We really had no intention of calling him, however had kept his card.

The morning we left for Los Angeles, we had stayed up most of the night (remember we were young then), we didn't have time to change clothes and had to get to the airport. We had a very early flight and we arrived at the airport in our finery from the night before; picture it – crinolines under party dresses, high heels, the jewelry, etc.

## FLYING HIGH

When we arrived in LA, we were not sure where we were going, so Loretta said, "Why not call the Mayor; it won't hurt." So I called him, and he said wait right there, go to landing strip ((I forget the number now) and I'll have John (his chauffeur) pick you up. About a half hour later we were taken to a landing strip by an airport security person and waited for John. Sure enough he landed, in a small private plane, and off we flew to Seal Beach, CA. It was around noon when we arrived at this lovely huge home in Seal Beach, with its own landing strip. It just so happened that there was a party going on with live entertainment. We met his lovely wife and many other guests and had just a fabulous time. Later on John brought us to a nice little Motel in Long Beach, where we stayed one-night and the next day we rented a lovely Beach House for the remainder of our stay. No, we weren't party girls just adventurous. Can you imagine doing that today? We weren't rich or famous but we sure felt important that day.

At the time, I worked for a Division Manager as a Secretary at Procter & Gamble in Hamilton, ON. While we were staying at the Beach House in California, we went to the beach where we met a group of Engineers from Procter & Gamble. When they found out that I worked for P & G in Hamilton, they asked us if we would like a tour of the plant in Long Beach. They arranged for a morning tour during the week and then we were invited to join them on a company bus trip to Tijuana, Mexico, the following Sunday to see the Bullfights.

We had a great day in Tijuana, but I did not like the Bull Fights; too much blood and gore and it was a steaming hot day in Tijuana. That California/Vegas trip turned out to be one of the best trips we ever had.

When we got home to Hamilton, I sent thank you cards to the Mayor, his chauffeur and the fine fellows that we met in Long Beach.

We had many more great trips before and after we all got married, e.g., Bermuda, Florida, Jamaica, Nassau, Acapulco, Mexico, New York City, Nashville, Tennessee, Branson, Missouri, Chicago, San Francisco, Texas, and the Eastern and Western Caribbean.

We all had good-paying jobs then. Carmen was at Tuckett's Tobacco Co. (no longer in Hamilton), Loretta worked at the American Can Co. (no longer in Hamilton) and I worked at Procter & Gamble (no longer in Hamilton). We all put money away for vacations and made sure we took one every year. I look back and think that was the best thing we ever did. We all got married in our mid to late 20s and all stayed married (we didn't need to find ourselves; we knew who we were). They really were the good old days, and I also believe we had the best music too; you could understand the words. Travelling was much easier then as well as safer.

**TRIP TO NASSAU, BAHAMAS**

In 1968, my husband, Len, and I took a trip to the Bahamas and stayed at a little efficiency *apartment/hotel in Cable Beach (where *Sir Harry Oakes once owned/stayed). I had been saving money for a trip for us because Len had never been on a plane or a 'real' holiday. When I told him that we had enough for a holiday to Nassau, he said "Why don't we stay home and pave the driveway?" "Pave the driveway", said I "forget that, we need a holiday, the driveway can wait." He really does not like to travel but we managed to have many good trips together, even a cruise, over the years. We owned a condo in Treasure Island, FL for 17 years, and he, our daughter Kelly and I enjoyed many wonderful family vacations down there.

**\*A bit of History and Mystery about Kirkland Lake, Ontario**

Sir Harry Oakes was a famous prospector and the founder of the Lake Shore Gold Mine in Kirkland Lake, ON. This mine was the second largest gold mine in North America and made Harry Oakes a very wealthy man. The Lake Shore mine also employed many fathers and sons in the town.

Sir Harry Oakes moved to the Bahamas in 1934, and in protest against the Canadian tax system, became a citizen of the Bahamas. In July, 1943, he was murdered in his home in Nassau and to this day, the murder has never been solved.

He did build a home in Kirkland Lake on the Lake Shore mine site for occasional visits (he actually lived in Niagara Falls, ON), and today the Harry Oakes Chateau houses the Kirkland Lake Museum of Northern History, a tourist attraction and a local landmark. I mention this story because I was born and raised in Kirkland Lake, graduated from the Kirkland Lake Collegiate and Vocational Institute, and moved to Hamilton when I was 18 years old. The Chateau, before it was refurbished, was a nursing home, and my father, who had Alzheimers, had a short stay there before he died in the Kirkland Lake District hospital on May 16, 1981, and my mother died eight months later on January 21, 1982. My father never worked in the gold mines but he did own his own cab business. I never knew until I left home that he also did a bit of bootlegging. I remember seeing him leave our house on occasional Sundays carrying a duffel bag. I asked my Mother what dad had in the bag, and she replied "Oh, he's going to the YMCA." Years later my mother told me he was delivering "mickies" (half bottles of liquor) to the Chief of Police, Fire Chief and sometimes to a few other prominent people in the town. Prohibition at its best in Kirkland Lake!

I had a wonderful childhood and wonderful parents and Kirkland Lake was a great place to grow up.

For those of you who do not know where Kirkland Lake is located (up North), I shall tell you. Heading up Highway 400 from Toronto, Highway 400 changes into Highway 11 about an hour north of Toronto. Drive for approximately three hours and you reach North Bay, then Cobalt, Haileybury, New Liskeard, and then not too much further up Highway 11, Earlton, then Englehart; just beyond Englehart, is Highway 112, the cutoff to Kirkland Lake.

**Kirkland Lake** was once known as the little town on the Mile of Gold. When I lived in K. L., there never was a lake. Years ago, Barrick Gold Corporation, the world's largest gold producer, bought up the old mine sites and started dredging for any remaining gold by-products, and a lake soon appeared on both sides of the road leading into Kirkland Lake. In 2001, Kirkland Lake Gold Inc., another mining company, took over the Lake Shore Mine, the Wright Hargreaves Mine, Teck Hughes Mine and Macassa

Mine, and these mines are again operating and producing gold. The former lakes are now but small ponds.

I do recall walking on the pipeline and playing with friends on the "slimes" located behind Weston's Bakery, which was located at the end of our street just before "the bush" where an old mine shaft was located. We would take off our shoes and walk barefoot on the "slimes" and pick up sparkles on our feet. The surface was flat and very smooth and sparkled in the sunlight – I guess we were walking on "gold dust". We thought that picking up the sparkles on our feet would bring us luck. I also remember my mother's warning to "Stay away from the mine shaft." We even took raw potatoes and would build a small fire, roast the potatoes and eat them by the mine shaft. We thought we were "prospectors" searching for gold. Great memories!

I must also mention that Kirkland Lake was known for producing many great National Hockey League players; over 40 of them were from Kirkland Lake.

Kirkland Lake was once a bustling community with a population of approximately 25,000, and today has a population of around 10,000, but perhaps holds a record for producing more NHL players and more retired gold miners per capita than any other place on earth.

A wonderful book was written by Richard Buell called *"The Glory of the Game"* and includes many stories and pictures of hockey heroes, history and heritage from The Mile of Gold. A great read for those who are interested in hockey and the good old days of the NHL.

**HOCKEY HERITAGE NORTH'S HONOURED MEMBERS FROM KIRKLAND LAKE**

| Player Name | Birthplace | Years in NHL | Cups |
| --- | --- | --- | --- |
| Backstrom, Ralph | Kirkland Lake, ON | 1956-1973 | 6 |
| Blackburn, Bob | Rouyn, PQ – Hometown – Kirkland Lake | 1968-1971 | |
| Blackburn, Don | Kirkland Lake, ON | 1962-1973 | |

| | | | |
|---|---|---|---|
| Boone, Carl "Buddy" | Kirkland Lake, ON | 1956-1958 | |
| Conacher, Roy | Toronto, ON – Hometown – Kirkland Lake | 1938-1952 | 2 |
| Connelly, Wayne | Rouyn, PQ – Hometown – Kirkland Lake | 1960-1972 | |
| Curry, Floyd | Chapleau, ON – Hometown – K. L. | 1947-1958 | 4 |
| Daoust Dan | Montreal, PQ – Hometown – Kirkland Lake | 1982-1990 | |
| Doran, John "Red" | Belleville, ON – Hometown – K. L. | 1933-1940 | |
| Duff, Dick | Kirkland Lake, ON | 1954-1972 | 6 |
| Durnan, Bill | Toronto, ON – Hometown – Kirkland Lake | 1943-1950 | 2 |
| Graboski, Tony | Timmins, ON – Kirkland Lake, ON | 1940-1943 | |
| Grosso, Don | Sault Ste. Marie – Hometown – K. L. | 1938-1947 | 1 |
| Hall, Murray | Kirkland Lake, ON | 1961-1972 | |
| Hamilton, Chuck | Kirkland Lake, ON | 1961-1973 | |
| Heiskala, Earl | Kirkland Lake, ON | 1968-1971 | |
| Hillman, Floyd "Bud" | Ruthevan, ON – Hometown – K. L. | 1956-1957 | |
| Hillman, Larry | Kirkland Lake, ON | 1954-1973 | 4 |
| Hillman, Wayne | Kirkland Lake, ON | 1960-1973 | 1 |
| Levandoski, Joe | Cobalt, ON | 1946-1947 | |
| Lindsay, Ted | Renfrew, ON – Hometown – Kirkland Lake | 1944-1965 | 4 |
| MacDonald, Kilby | Ottawa, ON – Hometown – Kirkland Lake | 1939-1945 | 1 |
| Marshall, Willie | Kirkland Lake, ON | 1952-1959 | |
| McLean, Kurtis | Kirkland Lake, ON | 2008 - | |
| McCreedy, Johnny | Winnipeg, MN – Hometown – K. L. | 1941-1945 | 2 |
| Mortson, Gus | New Liskeard, ON – Hometown K. L. | 1946-1959 | 4 |
| Murdoch, Bob | Kirkland Lake, ON | 1970-1982 | 2 |
| Noel, Claude | Kirkland Lake, ON | 1979-1980 | |
| Perry, Brian | Aldershot, England – Hometown – K. L. | 1968-1971 | |
| Plager, Barclay | Kirkland Lake, ON | 1967-1977 | |

| | | | |
|---|---|---|---|
| Plager, Bill | Kirkland, Lake, ON | 1967-1976 | |
| Plager, Bob | Kirkland Lake, ON | 1964-1978 | |
| Podolski, Nels | Winnipeg, MN – Hometown – K. L. | 1948-1949 | |
| Puppa, Daren | Kirkland Lake, ON | 1985-2000 | |
| Redmond, Dick | Kirkland Lake, ON | 1969-1982 | |
| Redmond, Mickey | Kirkland Lake, ON | 1967-1976 | 2 |
| Sloan, Bob | Kirkland Lake, ON | N/A | |
| Walton, Bob | Ottawa, ON – Hometown – Kirkland Lake | 1943-1944 | |
| Walton, Mike | Kirkland Lake, ON | 1965-1979 | 2 |
| Watson, Dave | Kirkland Lake, ON | 1979-1981 | |
| Watson, Jim | Malartic, PQ – Hometown – Kirkland Lake | 1963-1980 | |
| Webster, Tom | Kirkland Lake, ON | 1968-1980 | |

**Note: A total of 43 Cups were won with Kirkland Lake Players on the teams.**

Kirkland Lake now has the Hockey Heritage North museum, located on the Teck Hughes Mine property, where hockey memorabilia is on display for visitors to view. A huge hockey puck was installed (summer 2011) in the Hockey Heritage North Parking Lot. The puck is 12 ft. in diameter resting on a pedestal, and measures 20 ft. high, and was constructed by the Northern College A.A. &T. Welding students. All the money for this great project was raised through public donations to create this most fitting landmark and tourist attraction.

### Back to the Bahamas

While vacationing in Nassau, Len & I decided before leaving, that we would visit Paradise Island (where the one casino was located). We took a cab which cost $6.00 including the tip. We had $100 set aside for the evening; Len had $50 and I had $50. We played at a Blackjack table with a couple of Texas gentlemen, and I never forgot that experience because they were the most friendly and easy-going, fun-gamblers that I have had the pleasure to play with at a table. They did not complain when they were losing and treated gambling as a form of fun and entertainment. When we started to lose, we left the table and split up, and set a time to meet at the bar. I wandered around and watched the table games and then played a few quarter slot machines. It wasn't long before my money was gone; I had $1.50 left.

When I met Len at the bar, he had enough money left for us to have a beer and cab fare home. He said, "I wish we had enough for another beer," as we were enjoying the one we were having. I decided to go the Ladies Room before we caught a cab and on the way there, I saw a slot machine, thought, what the heck I'll put in 75 cents and call it a night. I put in the quarters, hit three 7s, and won $50. I rushed back to Len and said "Order another beer, I won $50!" On the way back from the washroom, I put in the other 75 cents and hit three 7s again, and won another $50! Now that was a win-win ending for our visit to the Casino, and a nice finish to our sun-filled vacation.

That evening we had the opportunity to watch two Texans at a crap table lose a lot of money but they still managed to have fun. They must have had the money to lose (maybe not) and it had to be very stressful for them, but they didn't show it at the crap tables (I'll Cry Tomorrow maybe)?

**PRAISE THE LORD**

When we left the casino it was just after midnight and we hailed a cab. When we got into the cab, the driver asked if we would mind waiting for his girlfriend, who was a cashier in the Casino. Her shift finished at midnight and did we mind if she rode with us, as she lived across the bridge near Cable Beach. No problem and we waited for her arrival. While we were waiting, "Jesus" our driver, started talking about the evils of gambling and how the Lord didn't put us here to partake in this form of entertainment. How interesting, I thought as Len and I glanced at each other a bit puzzled at his thought provoking comments. Shortly after this little lecture, his girlfriend "Angel" arrived and

Jesus introduced us to Angel, a pleasant young woman who cheerily said hello. She thanked us for waiting for her and settled in to talk to Jesus and then we are off to drive her home.

**Where in the Jungle are we?**

When we got across the Bridge, Jesus took a turn off the main road, and onto a winding road and now we were starting to feel a bit uneasy. We were getting further away from Cable Beach (we thought) and the road is dark and we are not seeing many lights. They were talking away in the front and we are feeling a bit frantic in the back. I then asked her if she gambled. Oh no, she said, "I just work at the casino, I do not gamble." Eventually we came to a small house; Angel said good night and thanked us for waiting, and Jesus walked her to the door. We are sitting in the back of the cab, in the middle of nowhere and thinking to ourselves, we really needed this little jaunt didn't we? Just then, Jesus jumps into the cab, continues with his "gambling lecture" and we finally got home. He thanked us for listening to him and waiting for Angel and then off he went. Now, isn't that a story and can you imagine us doing that today? How trusting were we? Yes, things were different then.

Today, if one wishes to gamble, it is not necessary to go to Las Vegas and other vacation spots worldwide as Casinos are now everywhere in Canada, the US and world-wide.

In 2002, I started to visit casinos with girlfriends approximately once every month or two. It would either be a day outing or an overnight visit. If going to the US, we would shop, check-into the hotel, have dinner and then hit the gaming floor. A couple of the girls played the slots while two of us played the tables. As for myself, I enjoyed the tables as I found your money went further. The slot machines were like vacuum cleaners. As of this writing, we still enjoy our junkets to the casino.

I personally set a limit for this type of entertainment outing and find that you must do this if you wish to enjoy the casino visit. A good idea is to keep a journal of money lost and won. If you are losing at a table game, try another game or slot machine or just leave. Remember, the casinos will still be there and you can always come back. I saw a sign posted in a casino that read: 'Sometimes the time to leave is when you win'. A very good suggestion.

**A FAULT RECOGNIZED IS HALF CORRECTED**

♣ ♦ ♥ ♠

# CHAPTER 2
# THE POSITIVE SIDE

**THE POSITIVE SIDE**

Seneca Niagara Casino opened on December 31, 2002. Shortly after the Nabisco Co. closed in Niagara Falls, NY, the Casino held a job fair at the Rainbow Mall and over 4,000 people showed up seeking employment. The Casino then set up a Dealer's School at the local Mall and training was provided for those who were hired. The training involved:

◊ Black Jack - 8 weeks

◊ Craps – 12 weeks

◊ Roulette – 10 weeks

◊ Caribbean Stud

◊ Let It Ride

◊ Pai Gow Poker

◊ 3 Card Poker

◊ Mississippi Stud

◊ Other – where training was needed, e.g., Poker Room

The Hotel opened in 2005. Today, there are approximately 3,800 people (full-time and part-time) employed by Seneca Casino properties. In-house training on table games and the Poker Room is an on-going process for new hires as well as other employees who apply for these positions. All job vacancies are posted and are open to any employee after 6 months of employment with the casino.

In June, 2010, I met with Joy Redeye, Director of Hotel Operations, whose responsibilities included the supervising of staff in the following areas of operation: Bell Men, Parking Attendants, Guest Services, Front-Line Reception, and Housekeeping. She was employed at Seneca Allegany from 2004 and moved to Seneca Niagara in April, 2008. She thoroughly enjoys her position and her responsibilities, which keep her very busy.

In August of 2010, I met with Tony Astran, Publicity Manager, Jim Kwasniak, Director of Employee Relations and Janet Crivello, Administrative Assistant, Housekeeping Dept. At this meeting, we discussed their job responsibilities as well as the contributions and employee involvement in the community.

**Team Member Benefits**

A number of programs are provided for Team Members of the Seneca Gaming Corporation. These programs include Social Security, Workers Compensation and Unemployment Insurance, as prescribed by law.

The Human Resources Department identifies programs for which Team Members are also eligible. The following benefit programs are available to those that are eligible:

Career Development

Company-sponsored activities*

Complimentary Team Member Meals*

Dental Coverage including orthodontia

Employee Assistance Program

Free Team Member Parking with Transportation provided

Medical Coverage with a comprehensive prescription program

Paid Time Off (PTO) including Vacation, Sick, Holidays, and Personal Time

Perfect Attendance Days Off

Pre-taxed Medical and Dependant Care Expense Accounts (Flex)

Promotion from Within*

Retirement Savings (401K)

Several Life Insurance Options including self and family plans

Short and Long-term Disability Insurance

Team Member Discounts*

Tuition Reimbursement Program

Uniforms and Maintenance of Uniforms provided

Vision Coverage

*available to all employees

As Director of Employee Relations, Jim deals with all employee issues, e.g. health issues, the Tuition Assistance Program (employees can apply in advance for assistance with tuition), i.e., English Language courses are encouraged for employees whose first language is not English (to assist them in their areas of employment). The casino reimburses their employees for successful completion of these language courses.

Publicity Manager, Tony, deals with public relations and the social media regarding entertainment and promotions, copywriting and social networking, i.e., Facebook and Twitter.

**A Special Media Event - Over the Edge** was held in July, 2010, and involved the participation of approximately 150 people, including casino personnel, rappelling over the edge of the 27-storey Hotel Tower. Each person raised

$1000 through pledges and over $100,000 was donated to the New York Special Olympics. Tony advised that another event is in the works for the summer of 2011. This Media Event is an audience-pleaser and truly a Winner!

Update: 2011 Over the Edge was held on July 29, and $150,000 was raised.

Note: Of course, all participants used practice walls with trainers, to prepare for this event.

An in-house program called Team Seneca Cares was set up to involve employee participation/volunteering for many community events and projects. Janet is very involved in this program and posts information for the on-going events. Employees sign up for events and incentives are offered for participation. This has proven to be a very successful program for everyone involved. These events include:

Employees volunteer on specific dates to literally clean up Niagara Falls from the Casino to the foot of the Falls every spring. This involves picking up garbage, taking it away and the sweeping up of the area.

Day of Caring – this event involved 20 – 40 Team Members volunteering their time to complete tasks for the agencies of the United Way. These tasks involved cleaning and helping to restore the boys and girls club of Niagara's County's camp site. They have given their time to the Salvation Army where they volunteer for cleaning, painting and fixing anything in need of repair. They also held a carnival in Hyde Park for the under-privileged children of Niagara Falls.

The culinary Staff volunteers each Thanksgiving and Christmas to cook meals for the Community Missions as well as sends food donations to the Niagara Falls Food Pantry.

The Human Resources Staff volunteer their time at the YMCA and assists with job placement, interviewing skills and resume writing.

Another side of community involvement is working with several organizations that aid those with developmental disabilities as well as physical handicaps. Their goal is to train their consumers along with help of the organizations, to give meaningful employment skills and assist them to become 'mainstreamed' into the workforce. A few of the organizations they have worked with include Opportunities Unlimited, United Cerebral Palsy, St. Mary's School for the Deaf and Hearing Impaired, and the Statler Foundation for the visually impaired.

The Casino/employee involvement and their work in these areas have been recognized by Niagara and Erie counties by receiving several awards from New York State.

During the course of a year, the Casino works with various fund-raising and volunteer activities, some on a corporate level and many on a personal or Team Member level. A partial list of groups are: Cradle Beach, Roswell Park Cancer Institute, Multiple Sclerosis Society, Women and Children's Hospital of Buffalo, American Red Cross (Blood Donor clinics are held), Make A Wish Foundation, Special Olympics, Variety Kids Telethon, Haitian and Katrina Relief Funds (two semi-trailers with donated goods, water and other supplies were donated to victims of Hurricane Katrina), United Way, Locks of Love, Project Linus (Handmade blankets for Hope by team members), Community Missions, Firemen's Toy Drive, Juvenile Diabetes Research Foundation and the Lupus Foundation.

From the Team Member Newsletter:

**Be of service. Whether you make yourself available to a friend or co-worker, or you make time every month to do volunteer work, there is nothing that harvests more of a feeling of empowerment than being of service to someone in need.**

**Gillian Anderson**

**Employee Rewards**

When employees participate in 8 events, they are rewarded with a day off with pay.

2009 was a record-breaking year for Team Seneca Cares. This was the second year of the program and 30 days with pay was awarded; more importantly, 2700 hours of community service was contributed by the employees.

Outstanding employees are recognized with Employee of the Year awards, a Heart of the House Award, Sterling Cup Awards (looks like miniature Stanley Cup and are awarded regularly to employees based on casino guest feedback).

Employee Appreciation Days are held as are 4-Diamond Celebration days; these could include Staff Bar-B-Q's, Picnics and other venues where gifts, prizes and other awards are presented.

The Casino involvement in community events is low-key; the Casino does not do this for recognition but as it is an integral part of employment with the casino, they offer many incentives to get the employees involved which benefits both staff and the community.

Seneca Niagara has won the 4-Diamond Award from 2006 to 2011, awarded by the American Automobile Association (Triple AAA Award).

Mickey Brown, (a former CEO) made this statement:

**"WE WILL MAKE A DIFFERENCE IN THIS COMMUNITY"**

Note: Several employees who opened with Seneca Niagara/Allegany are still there today and continue to enjoy employment with this employer.

**DO WHAT YOU CAN TODAY, YOU MAY NOT HAVE THE SAME OPPORTUNITY TOMORROW**

♣ ♦ ♥ ♠

## CHAPTER 3
## EMPLOYMENT IN THE GAMING INDUSTRY

# EMPLOYMENT IN THE CASINO INDUSTRY

Today it is not unusual for individuals to hold down two or three jobs because of the floundering economy. The fact that many companies hire by contract and do not choose to pay into employee pension plans or pay for health and other benefits has created this workplace environment.

Employment is rapidly growing in the service industry and one popular area is in the gaming area. The industry offers many forms of employment, one of which is the casino industry.

Casinos provide employment opportunities for individuals with specific job skills required for the numerous jobs that must be filled in running a casino. Here is a list of jobs that must be filled for the successful running of a casino/s:

Bartender and Cocktail Servers

Fine Dining Servers

Cage Cashiers/Cage Shift Supervisors

Waiters and Waitresses

Restaurant Hostesses/Hosts

Dining Area Cashiers

Culinary Chefs/Cooks

Emergency Paramedics

Front Desk Agents

Bell Captain

Bellhops/luggage handlers

Parking Attendants

Security Officers (inside and outside premises)

Public Area Attendants

Housekeeping Manager

Guest Room Attendants

Laundry personnel

Kitchen Workers

Maintenance Technicians (general maintenance of the casino/hotel building and grounds)

Electricians/Mechanics/Plumbers

Human Resource Manager

Floor Bosses/Shift Managers/Supervisors

Project Managers

Dealers (needed for all games except the slots)

Slot Technicians

Note: Dealers receive a share of 'chip tips' given by the table players; these tips are collected once a shift and are shared by the table dealers on each shift. These tip-amounts are then added to their regular pay-checks.

Floor personnel (for player assistance/Jackpot payouts)

Money counters/chip counters

Accountants

Finance

Promotion Manager/s

Publicity Manager/s

Casino Hosts/Hostesses

Promotion desk personnel (for Player assistance/inquiries)

Event Planners/Entertainment

Marketing Manager/s

Legal Department

Administration (Top Management positions)

Web Developers/Social Media

Retail Clerks (Gift shop/s)

Spa Salon/Receptionist/Stylist

Note: Most positions require a High School Diploma or equivalency and must be 18 years of age or older upon employment.

Casino employees are not allowed to gamble in the casino where they are employed.

You must be 21 years of age to gamble in the US.

The casinos run 24/7; this requires 3 shifts which involves the hiring of additional full-time and part-time employees to cover all shifts.

**OTHER AREAS OF EMPLOYMENT WORTH EXPLORING**

**CRUISE LINES**

This is an area that continues to grow in the Travel Industry, and I have had the good fortune to take a few cruises. One Caribbean cruise with my husband, Len, an Eastern Caribbean Cruise, with a long-time friend Marian, from Kirkland Lake, ON, one with my dear daughter, Kelly; we cruised the Western Caribbean, and an Alaskan cruise with another dear friend, Alice, (now deceased).

The cruise ships all had casinos and were just another form of entertainment on board.

I spoke with a few of the dealers on these cruises, and they were from everywhere. The younger ones worked the cruise ships on a part-time basis while going to school to further their education. The older ones loved this form of employment and had worked in the cruise industry for many years, doing various jobs. They all spoke at least two, three or more languages, which they said helped them procure their jobs, and they all said it was a great way to see the world. It also gave them the opportunity to practice their English and communication skills and to meet people from all over the world.

**GAMING DESIGN**

The gaming design area is a huge area for employment and exploration.

In the past, slot machine gaming consisted of bars, bells and cherries. Today, there are hundreds of various slot machine games to play, ranging from one cent, two-cents, and 5-cents to $100 or higher. The players like a variety of slot play and that is why new games are always being created and introduced to the gaming floor.

As reported in *The Hamilton Spectator, June 27, 2011*: In Hamilton, Ontario, two brothers Colin and Greg Ferguson, and colleague Chris Burr started their own company called Snakehead Games Inc. This company has created world-renowned online video games, and as Colin stated "It's a virtual business."

In 2008, the company released *Star Pirates*, its flagship game. This game was partly created through their passion for *Dungeons and Dragons*, which they played when they were 12-year olds. This game was designed for short work breaks or a stress release for office workers." Colin emphasized that they are not encouraging "slackers"; the game is just to be used for minimal breaks from their regular work. They even have secret log-ins that appear as regular websites, e.g., Wikipedia.

*Snakehead Games are free but players can buy points (with real money) to speed up the game; they do not have any advertising on their site. Points can be purchased, e.g., 5,000 points for $30. A typical game can use only three or five points at a time, which allows their point-purchase to last for awhile. Their company funding comes from the purchase of points by the players.

*When I asked Colin if this was not a form of gambling, he said, "The purpose of their company is not to promote gambling." My thoughts on this are: where money is exchanged for points to play any type of game, is really another form of gambling.

Their company has been contacted by soldiers on tour in Afghanistan as well as other individuals with serious illnesses who play the online game and all players are treated equally. This is another form of social media where gamers interact on line and share their stories. Success of this form of social media can also be attributed to two of their players who met up in real life and are now married.

To date, they have attracted more than 100,000 gamers. See:

www.snakeheadgames.com

www.starpirates.net

www.spybattle.net

Colin, a social media expert, works on his laptop in an office in Hamilton, while Greg and Chris, handle the programming out of a Brantford, Ontario, location.

Colin's definition of 'social media': "The digitization of public communication."

They collaborated with McMaster Innovation Park, in Hamilton, to enhance their entrepreneurial skills which led to their on-going success in the gaming-design industry.

Note: McMaster Innovation Park is very involved in architecture, cinema, dance, music, painting, poetry, and sculpture. Among other things, McMaster wants to become a gaming and digital media hub.

Mo Elbestawi, McMaster's Vice President of research, hopes that this institute will attract students, and researchers, which will result in opportunities for internships and future employment opportunities.

At the end of our interview, I suggested that perhaps they should be looking into the Casino gaming design industry for future endeavors.

For additional information on their success story: mhayes@thespec.com *(Brothers' video games attract players from around the globe).*

## EMPLOYMENT IN THE GAMING INDUSTRY – The Interviews

### Job Position: Table Games/Floor Supervisor

I was able to interview Charles Dunkle otherwise known as Uncle Dunkle to friends and relatives. Charles has been with Seneca Niagara Casino for over 9 years and now holds the position of a Floor Supervisor. He is a very pleasant man and his pleasant attitude and rapport with customers is evident when he is on the job.

As a Supervisor, he is responsible for the efficient operation of the Table Games on an assigned shift. All duties are to be performed within the guidelines of the Corporation's policies, procedures, Internal Control Standards and objectives.

### Essential Functions and Responsibilities

◊ Monitor controls designed to assure full compliance with state, federal, and tribal regulatory requirements

◊ Maintain a continuous inspection of cards and dice, ensuring the security of the Table Games at all times

◊ Assist in monitoring the payouts on the table games to ensure that proper amounts are being paid to customers

◊ Monitor transactions between dealers and patrons

◊ Monitor any and all unusual activity

◊ Utilize effective communication tools to ensure that accurate and timely information is provided throughout a shift

◊ Provide customer service to all patrons and communicate in a pleasant, friendly and professional manner at all times.

The Floor Supervisor reports to the Pit Manager.

**Qualifications/Requirements**

**Education/Experience**

◊ High School diploma or equivalent required

◊ Must demonstrate leadership, fairness, and sensibility to the customers and employees, and a positive attitude.

**Language Skills and Reasoning Ability**

◊ Must possess communication skills/speak effectively to the public, employees and customers

◊ Must have the ability to deal effectively and interact well with well customers and employees.

**Physical Requirements and Work Environment**

◊ The noise level in the work environment is usually moderately loud; when on the casino floor, the noise levels increase to loud

◊ Must be able to work in an environment where *smoking is permitted

*There is a non-smoking section called Turtle Island at Seneca Niagara Casino, Niagara Falls, NY.

Reasonable accommodations may be made to enable individuals with disabilities to perform the essential functions of the job.

For additional career opportunities and job titles/requirements, see website:

www.senecagamingcorporation.com/careers.cfm

**Casino Myth:** "Fresh air is being continually pumped into the atmosphere to keep players alert or awake." Not true: the Casino ventilation system activates at regular intervals just like any pubic system. Where smoking is permitted, the system is more active.

### Honor Flight Buffalo

While Charles enjoys his job as a Floor Supervisor, he is also the Chief Executive Officer of an organization called Honor Flight Buffalo. This organization is a Not-For-Profit Public Charity Organization. Seneca Niagara Casino contributes to this organization and, of course, their contribution is greatly appreciated.

As this book's main content is about the gaming industry, I chose to include data on Honor Flight Buffalo based on Charles' commitment and dedication to this organization. I hope readers enjoy this diversion to another area of interest.

Co-founded by Charles Dunkle*, CEO, Jo-Anne Wylie, Vice President, and Lisa A. Wylie, President, after serving as volunteer 'Guardians' on an Honor Flight in 2008, they soon realized the organization's national office had greater than 300 World War II veterans in the Buffalo area waiting to make the journey to Washington to see their memorial. In 2009, Honor Flight Buffalo became the 95th 'official' hub of the Honor Flight Network serving Erie, Niagara and surrounding counties area vets. There are greater than 95 Honor Flight Hubs nationally and approximately 50,000 war vets are registered. The Honor Flight Network has flown over 85,000 vets to Washington.

The mission of Honor Flight Buffalo and the Honor Flight Network is to fly America's veterans, at no charge, to Washington, DC to visit those memorials dedicated to honor their sacrifices. Top priority is given to America's most senior Veterans – survivors of WWII and any veteran with a terminal illness who wishes to visit the memorial. Current statistics indicate that America is losing these heroes at a rate of 900 each day. Next priority is the

Korean War Veterans, then the Viet Nam Veterans and will continue in chronological order of other conflicts.

Each year Honor Fight Buffalo flies local veterans to Washington, at no charge, to visit the Washington Memorial. The cost to send one Veteran is $375. In the 2010 Flying Season, 55 WWII veterans (also referred to as the Greatest Generation) travelled to Washington. Five flights have been scheduled for 2011.

Grand Island High School, NY is the first school to support Honor Flight Buffalo. Principal, Sandra Anzalone, stated that "Our students and staff have truly embraced the opportunity to thank those who have served our community." Through creative fund-raising, Grand Island high school raised enough money to sponsor a visit to Washington, DC for four local veterans. On May 21, 2011, two student guardians were the first Grand Island High School students to accompany veterans from western New York on the flight to Washington. What a great endeavor and now that the younger generation is involved, this makes this organization even more special.

*Charles' children, Matt and Lauren are also on the Board of Directors

Other Facts

◊ World War II was a global conflict that took place from 1939 to 1945

◊ Historically marked as the deadliest military conflict, over 60 million people lost their lives

◊ Over 16 million Americans served in World War II and close to 400,000 died during the war

◊ Honor Flight Buffalo's hub has a waiting list of 200 vets

◊ Approximately 900 American World War II veterans die every day

◊ The median age for a World War II Veteran in February, 2009 was 86 years

◊ Sky-rocketing health care costs have drained the life savings of most WWII veterans and their spouses

◊ Veterans of World War II have waited over 59 years for their memorial. Most of them have been unable to visit the memorial until now.

As of this writing, more than one million people have visited the Washington War Memorial.

A quote from the organization:

**"If you can read this thank a teacher. If you can read this in English, thank a WWII veteran before it's too late!"**

For additional information: www.Honor FlightBuffalo.org

NATIVE AMERICAN HERITAGE MONTH
November 1 – 30, 2011

In June, 2002, Congress passed the Code Talkers Recognition Act. This act recognized the important part that American Indians played in "performing highly successful communications operations of a unique type that greatly assisted in saving countless lives and in hastening the end of World War I and World War II." The Act recognizes the Native American contributions to the U.S. war efforts during World War I and World War II despite social discrimination against them.

In Canada, it is estimated that more than 7000 First Nations people served in the First and Second World Wars and the Korean War and an unknown number of Inuit, Métis and other native peoples also participated.

On June 1, 2001, Governor General Adrian Clarkson unveiled the National Aboriginal Veterans War Monument in Ottawa, Canada.

**NOTE:** In 1964, while employed with the Federal Government in Ottawa, Canada, I was a Stenographer II in the Department of External Affairs. At that time, I saw Native land claims attached to Land Surveys that were delivered to the Department. They were date-stamped and then delivered to the Department of Indian and Northern Affairs (I think that was the title of the Department at that time). When I asked a colleague, "Where do the land claims go from there"? I was told "Oh, we just file them."

Perhaps, if the land claims were dealt with then, we would not be experiencing the many unresolved issues with the Native Land Claims today.

### Canadian Virtual War Memorial

As I am Canadian, I am including a reference to the Canadian Virtual War Memorial (CVWM) website. www.Canadian Virtual War Memorial.org

This website contains a registry of information about the graves and memorials of more than 116,000 Canadians and Newfoundlanders who served valiantly and gave their lives for their country. Included on this site are the memorials of more than 1500 soldiers who died in service to Canada since the Korean War, including personal memorabilia about individual Canadians. The purpose of the Canadian Virtual War Memorial is to recognize and keep alive the memory of the achievements and sacrifices made by those who served Canada in the defense of freedom and so have contributed to the development as Canada as a nation.

The memorial is a project of Industry Canada and Veterans Affairs Canada.

**Note:** My uncle Ray served in World War II and while he was stationed in Holland, he sent all his nieces and nephews little wooden shoes from Holland. I still have those little shoes. When he returned home from overseas, he built a lovely home for his wife and daughter. Shortly after, he took his own life. My father said he never got over the war and my uncle told him he had terrible nightmares. He said "War is Hell."

My father also told me that he sent Uncle Ray a "mickie" of Rye in a hollowed out loaf of bread. He did receive it and he said he and his buddies really enjoyed a "yank of Rye" as my father called it.

## KOREAN WAR – 1950 – 53

As reported in the *Hamilton Spectator*, Oct. 31, 2011, by Guy Black.

The U.S. Department of Defense formed a commemorative committee to mark the 60th Anniversary of the Korean War. The committee wants to bestow an official commemorative certificate on all Korean War veterans from allied countries.

Canada's contingent of volunteers was successful in helping to restore peace but the toll was high, amounting to 516 war dead. An estimated 10 million soldiers and civilians from both sides of the 38th parallel had been killed.

Since the war, the Republic of Korea and its citizens, many who have immigrated to Canada, continually show their great admiration and thanks for what Canadians did for them.

The United States Department of Defense is looking for all veterans of the Korean War. If you are a veteran of the Korean War and would like to receive the Department of Defense Commemorative Certificate, please contact committee member:

Guy Black, 944 Dundonald Drive, Port Moody, B.C., V3H1B7 or email: korea19501953@yahoo.com

Guy Black is a recipient, Minister of Veterans Affairs Commendation, an honorary member, Korea Veterans Association of Canada, and the Korea Veterans Association Western Canada Chapter.

He states: Our Promise to our Korean War Heroes is:

**"We will remember those that will forever remain on the Korean Peninsula, and we will never forget the great struggle to restore peace."**

For a very interesting and informative read: Triumph at Kapyong by Author Dan B. Bjarnason. His book tells the story of what he calls "the forgotten war or Citizens war";

he tells the amazing story of the Canadian contingent in the battle at Kapyong.

From the U.S. Air Force Fact Sheet:

**APPRECIATION MAKES PEOPLE FEEL MORE IMPORTANT THAN ALMOST ANYTHING YOU CAN GIVE THEM**

**Lest We Forget**

**In Flanders Fields**

In Flanders fields the poppies blow

Between the crosses, row on row,

That mark our place: and in the sky

The larks still bravely singing fly

Scarce heard amid the guns below.

We are the dead: Short days ago,

We lived, felt dawn, saw sunset glow,

Loved and were loved: and now we lie

In Flanders fields!

Take up our quarrel with the foe

To you, from failing hands, we throw

The torch: be yours to hold it high

If ye break faith with us who die,

We shall not sleep, though poppies grow

In Flanders fields.

By Canadian Lieutenant Colonel John McCrae

## Job Position: Bartender

We had the pleasure of meeting Frank, an award-winning bartender at the Seneca Niagara Casino in Niagara Falls, NY

Frank has been in the bartending business for over 33 years. He has been a casino bartender for 10 years and has been with Seneca Niagara for 9 years and has the distinction of being the opening bartender for the award-winning Western Door Steakhouse at Seneca. He is very friendly and personable and was honored with the distinction of Employee of the Year at the Seneca Alleghany Casino in Salamanca, NY.

"Monsignor Ryan/Father Ryan" (as Frank is called by his coworkers), because of his knowledge and experience as one of the top bartenders in the business, is very involved in his trade. He is instrumental in the training of other bar/restaurant employees and loves his job. He encourages staff to learn something new every day by attending seminars to learn more about mixology and to expand their knowledge of the various brands available for the bar business.

What he enjoys most about his job is that no day is ever the same. He meets many interesting people, a few of whom are celebrities and pro-athletes in the fine-dining restaurants at Seneca.

What he enjoys least about his job is the late hours and working the holidays which takes him away from family on special occasions. However, he feels the good outweighs the bad and accepts this as part of his job.

The pay is excellent and the tips are very good. As well, there are great opportunities for career advancement in the Casino industry.

I asked Frank if he hears any winning/losing stories from his customers. He has heard many stories but of course cannot discuss because of the confidentiality agreement with his employer.

From what he has seen, more women gamble than men on slots/poker machines.

Frank likes to go to Las Vegas once or twice a year and likes the Bellagio casino. He also visits the smaller or local casinos and believes the pay-offs are better. He plays table games, e.g., Blackjack and video poker.

What he looks for when he visits a casino is nice restaurants, a great bar atmosphere and likes to be comfortable with the people/players at table games. I certainly agree with him on being comfortable with the people at table games. I have left tables where a negative player/s complains about the cards, the dealer, etc. I never even think of the four-letter word 'Lose' for an outing at a casino, because a positive attitude and thinking 'Win" makes for a much more pleasant experience.

Frank believes that you should always listen to the customer and strive to make their visit pleasant so they will return. Frank has many customers that return to see him at the bar when they visit the casino.

Frank has won awards and has had his special drinks published in national bartending magazines. For seven years he wrote many columns (Behind the Bar and Ask an Expert) that were published in the Buffalo News and Niagara Falls Gazette. He was also chosen as Bartender of the Year in the local entertainment newspaper for the Niagara region's weekly eat-out-and-go guide.

It was such a pleasure meeting Frank and I would like to share a few of his signature cocktail recipes below:

**Frank's Specialty Drinks**

**Seneca Sweetheart Martini**

2 oz. Bacardi Grand Melon Rum

1 oz. DeKuyper Watermelon Schnapps

2 oz. Pomegranate Juice

Sugar rim of martini glass, shake the ingredients

Strain into glass

Garnish with an apple peel

**Crystal Clementine**

2 oz. Svedka Clementine Vodka

½ oz. Dekuyper Cherri-Berry Schnapps

2 oz. fresh-squeezed Orange Juice

Sugar rim of martini glass with cherry-orange flavored color sugar

Shake and strain

Garnish with orange curly twist

**Blue-Doo Child Martini**

2 oz. Stoli Blueberry Vodka (Russian)

½ oz. DeKuyper Tropical Mango Liqueur

2 oz. Pineapple Juice

Shake with ice, strain into martini glass

Drizzle ¼ oz. Blue Curacao into glass

(Blue Curacao will sink to bottom)

Garnish with Pineapple slice

**The Wave**

1 oz. Bacardi Grand Melon Rum

2 oz. Medori Melon Liqueur

Splash of Pineapple Juice

1 oz. Coco Lopez Liqueur

¼ oz. Grenadine

Mix all contents in blender with ice (must be frozen). Pour into Tulip or Hurricane Glass

Garnish with Pineapple and Cherry

**Tuscany Sour**

1 oz. Tuscany (Italian Orange Liqueur)

1 oz. Frangelico Hazel Nut Liqueur

2 oz. Sweet and sour mix

Shake and pour contents (ice as well) into a Hurricane glass; float ½ oz. Chianti (red wine), on

Top; garnish with an orange twist and cherry

**007 Martini (an old Classic) and my favorite**

1 oz. Grey Goose Vodka

1 oz. Gin

1 drop Vermouth

Pour into shaker over a cup of ice; vigorously shake and pour into a Martini glass; add a twist of

Lemon or an olive/s if requested.

Note: Having tasted a few Martinis over the years, Frank makes the perfect 007 Martini.

**There is nothing like a good "Happy Hour" also known as an "Attitude Adjustment Hour".**

**Trivia: (Questions and Answers from Frank's many columns)**

1. Why do they call the restaurant you work in "the Western Door"?

Of the Mohawk, Oneida, Onondaga, Cayuga and the Seneca tribes, the Seneca's are the most western tribe; the Seneca's are the keepers or protectors of the "Western Door." The Mohawks are the most eastern.

2. What does VSOP means on a brandy bottle?

VSOP is usually found on cognac. It means 'very special old pale' and the cognac (brandy) is at least 4-1/2 years old.

3. What is the difference between ale and a lager?

Ale is top-fermented, which means the yeast hangs out at the top of the tank. Lager is bottom-fermented, meaning, the yeast remains at the bottom of the tank during fermentation.

4. What does aperitif mean?

Derived from the French word appetizer, which means to open; the aperitif is the first drink served before a meal.

5. Who makes the best pinot grigio?

The Italians, says Frank, and "you can take that to the bank." Be sure your pinot label reads Trentino or Della Venezia on the label.

6. What makes a wine that is said to be kosher different from standard wines?

Taste-wise, nothing. When kosher wine is in production, only religiously observant Jews may touch the product or equipment at the winery, and only kosher items may be used in the wine-making process.

7. When pouring a beer, how much head should be on the top?

Experts say the head on the top should be equal to the width of two fingers. However, some patrons do not like a head on their beer, so it is best to know your customers.

8. What is kir?

Kir is chilled dry white wine with a teaspoon Crème de Cassis (a liqueur made from fruits and berries). A Kir Royale would be made with champagne instead of white wine. Many younger people are mixing Chambord Black Raspberry Liqueur with champagne and calling it Kir.

9. What does the term 'potato vodka mean?

It simply means that the vodka was distilled with potatoes instead of grain. I feel Poland makes the best potato vodka.

10. Can you use beer to draw snails and slugs away from your flowers and plants?

Absolutely, says Frank: Pour a beer into a dish or pan. Sink it in the ground away from your flowers. The snails and slugs are attracted to the yeast smell of the beer. Slugs love beer. When they go in for a drink; they will drown.

Notes from Frank:

If you ever pass through Kentucky or Tennessee, visit the Jim Bean or Jack Daniel's distilleries. You will thoroughly enjoy the visit as well as learn a few things.

Notice the different spellings the Canadian and Scotch use—they spell the spirit 'whisky'. The Irish and Americans spell it whiskey. In addition, in Britain, the term whisky means Scotch whisky unless otherwise specified. Americans think of whiskey Kentucky Bourbon, Canadian Rye or Tennessee sour mash.

**THE NICE THING ABOUT TEAMWORK IS THAT YOU ALWAYS HAVE OTHERS ON YOUR SIDE**

FRANK RYAN - AWARD WINNING BARTENDER

**Job Position: Dealer**

**Las Vegas, NV**

**June and I**

In June, 2009, I met with Robert C., a dealer at the Flamingo Las Vegas Hotel. Robert was a Policeman in Orange County, CA for 3-1/2 years before moving to Las Vegas in 1985. He was a dealer for 2-1/2 years at the Western Hotel on Freemont Street in downtown Las Vegas. He has been at the Flamingo for over 25 years. He works the day-shift, with weekends off. The wages are very good, the table tips for the shift are split between the dealers and he averages approximately $26/hr. per 8-hr. shift or $45,000/yr. He is eligible for 6 weeks paid vacation annually, is fortunate to have covered parking for his car which is a bonus with the Las Vegas heat. There is no Union and employees can collect up to 30 sick days for full pay. There is a Merit Program and Salary Grid Evaluation. He thoroughly enjoys his job.

He has been married for 33 years. He went to grade school with his 'gal' and together they went to high school. They have three children, live in a nice home in outer Las Vegas and he loves the climate and living in Las Vegas.

**A Flamingo Story:** The Casino was robbed about 11 years ago, around 10 or 11 p.m. Apparently, 4 men walked up to Cashier Cage Shift Manager, held a gun to his head, got $300,000, left through the front circular door, sped down the alleyway by the Tropicana, The Riviera and Harrah's. The ground cameras saw them, but the Security Guards were not armed, the robbers got away and have never been caught.

Update: September, 2011

On this visit, we were told by a Security Guard who has worked for the Casino for over 25 years that two of the men were finally caught this year.

## SECURITY — LOST and FOUND

I had the opportunity to chat with a Security Guard whose name was Johnny. I asked him if he liked his job and he said he loved it; he loved meeting the people. He also told me about the many items that are left behind in the rooms, the elevators, washrooms, and the lobby.

People forget their luggage; they leave laptops in the elevator and at the checkout desk, and on the gaming floor. Eyeglasses, sunglasses, shoes, clothing left in closets, jewelry left in drawers, medications, assortment of articles left at the pool, etc., are found on a regular basis. Canes and even strollers have been left at the casino.

He has seen it all. His best story was about a set of false teeth left in a cup, and of a lady who left her walker in the room. When asked how she forgot her walker, she replied "Oh, I only use it when I lose!"

Hundreds of items are turned in daily. The items are bagged and dated, and if left in the room, the room number is written on the bag. The bagged items are sent to Lost and Found where they are logged in a book. People have 30 days to claim the items and the items that are not claimed within the time limit are donated or thrown out.

I left my cell-phone in a room once, and when I notified the hotel, they took my name and address and it was sent back to me by Fed Ex. I had it back within 24 hours. That was service at its best!

## CRAFTY CORA

Cora, a Security Guard at Seneca Niagara is a very delightful and interesting person. Cora's station is just outside the elevators at the casino. She makes all kinds of little crafty things, e.g., dime on a ring (diamond ring). Dime on a pin (diamond pin), mini-dice rings, pins, earrings, magnets, etc. She greets the guests as they get off/on the elevators, and gives these little gifts to them. When asked why she does this? She replied, "I just love people and like to make them smile." She loves her job and works week-days with weekends off. She alone pays for her craft material and expects nothing in return except a smile.

She also checks that people entering the elevator area have hotel room cards and are registered guests in the hotel.

We have seen Cora and other Security personnel do some very special things for people, e.g., assisting with the handicapped and children or interpreting directions/language issues. They do a fine job and it is always appreciated when one is greeted with a smile.

NOTE:

Security can locate an individual's location in the casino if that individual has inserted their player's card into a slot machine or if he/she has submitted the player's card for registering at a gaming table. As mentioned previously, players do use their playing card for the accumulation of points for rewards and promotions).

## HOW MUCH YOU LOVE LIVING SHOWS IN YOUR LIFE

*Nora & Ken,*
*my friends are my family. Enjoy life with a smile.*
*Cora*

♣ ♦ ♥ ♠

# CHAPTER 4
# THE OTHER SIDE

**THE OTHER SIDE**

During July, 2010, while dining at the Western Door Steakhouse at Seneca Niagara, my friend Marnie and I had the good fortune to meet a most interesting server. During our short-conversations between courses, I mentioned that I was writing a book on gambling and was looking for additional information on the positive side of the casino industry. He gave me his card and he said he had some material that I might be interested in. From there, his great story grew, and we also found a wonderful friend.

**Meet Hal Limebeer from Buffalo, NY**

Hal is in his late forties and has been employed with Seneca Niagara Casino since October, 2005. His story really begins with a rebuttal article he wrote in August, 2006, which was published online on *Buffalo Rising* at www.buffalorising.com. Hal's lengthy essay was in response to numerous articles (but most indignantly to the article in v5, n3, January 19, 2006, published in *Artvoice and* written by Bruce Jackson, a Professor at the University at Buffalo; his article was against the Casino/s and gaming industry. Hal has given permission to use his response which is now 'public information'.

**Jackpot! A Casino Employee Speaks Up (And Trumps all Those Little White Lies & Big, Bold Lies) by Hal. A. Limebeer, August, 2006.**

I have read, and re-read, many articles written about the Seneca Gaming Corporation and their casino operations (both completed and proposed), in *Artvoice and the Buffalo News;* I would like the opportunity to correct some of the information that has been stated as fact, which is, in fact, not true. The mother lode of what I have read was written by Bruce Jackson in *Artvoice*. However, before I get into all of the issues, let me make some full disclosures up front: I am an employee of Seneca Gaming Corporation (SGC), and am employed at Seneca Niagara Casino.

I am not a spokesman for SGC, or the Seneca Nation of Indians (SNI). I have not requested permission to submit this response. However, I do feel uniquely qualified to respond to some of what Mr. Jackson has stated. BECAUSE of the fact that I am one of 'the little people', and, as such, some readers may be inclined to read something, and judge it objectively, written by someone who is not being paid to respond to such articles.

Some statements made by Mr. Jackson are what I would call 'Little White Lies', like referring to the Seneca Niagara Casino as a 'windowless' building. Apparently, Mr. Jackson hasn't been to the casino. There is a very long wall of windows that covers almost the entire second floor front of the casino, facing west. At any time, you can look up and be able to discern 'daytime' from 'nighttime'. A minor point, but it is now corrected. Many other of Mr. Jackson's statements are more along the lines of 'Big, Bold Lies'.

More disclosures: A few years ago, I was a waiter at a restaurant on Elmwood Avenue for a time, and had occasion to serve Mr. Jackson. He was always charming and engaging. And always a great tipper. Thank you Mr. Jackson. Since then, in the 3 years immediately preceding my employment with the SGC, I was a waiter at a downtown (Franklin Street) restaurant. And, for what it's worth, I usually purchase gas at Allentown Trading Company, a business owned by Carl Paladino. It's close, convenient, and clean. Now on with my response.

As I read Mr. Jackson's 'Casino Chronicles #1' in *Artvoice* (v5n3, January 19, 2006), I came across this statement. "If they set up a whorehouse that will be tax-exempt too." I was immediately offended by this sentence. I believe I would be offended by such a statement even if I was not a Seneca employee. For the record, I am not Native American, but, if I was, I no doubt suspect I would be EVEN MORE OFFENDED. What an outrageous and offensive comment to make. The fact that it simply is not plausible for the SGC to do what Mr. Jackson states is enough to write this off as the inflammatory rhetoric that it is.

Before I address a few other matters in Mr. Jackson's articles, let me also state that the day before my interview with the SGC (October 2005), there was a letter in the *Buffalo News* 'Everybody's Column', written by a doctor from Williamsville. In it, the good doctor stated that the casino jobs in Niagara Falls, did not, in fact, come with the good pay and benefits that I happened to be applying for. The doctor specifically stated, as I recall, that "only about 200 jobs" are full-time with benefits.

I took the article with me to the interview. How am I to know what the truth is? It was written by a doctor! From Williamsville! Letters like that, and articles like Mr. Jackson's, constantly claim to know the facts. Time to set a few 'facts' straight.

First, I was assured by the man who interviewed me (Kevin Young) that casino employees were expected to be full-time, unless otherwise clearly stated, and the full-time positions have benefits. The position I was applying for (a server at the Western Door: A Seneca Steakhouse) was, in fact, full-time with benefits. To my knowledge, all the servers, and in fact nearly everyone I have met so far at Seneca Niagara, are full-time employees, with benefits. Let's talk about that, shall we?

Lowest wage/Lowest Benefit?

Mr. Jackson states that casino jobs are those with the 'lowest wage/lowest benefit' and the jobs at Seneca Buffalo Creek Casino will somehow displace better-paid workers who currently have benefits. Oh really? A front page article in *The Buffalo News* dated Sunday, April 16, 2006, stated: 'More than 3,050 people work at the casino complex earning an average of $28,000 a year with $8,400 in fringe benefits.' It also states, 'The casino, through its spending and its employees' spending, may be responsible for another 1,000 local jobs, notably vendors serving the casino.'

Prior to my employment at the casino, and after 3 years at one of Buffalo's top restaurants, I was still making $3.85 per hour, and I had zero paid benefits. My healthcare, which I paid out of pocket, was over $280 per month. Single coverage. When my benefits kicked in at the casino, on March 1, my out-of-pocket costs dropped to just over $15 per week, and now included healthcare, dental, eyeglasses and life insurance. For the record, I started at the Casino as a server, at $5.25 per hour; not $3.85 per hour as was standard at nearly every restaurant in Buffalo (I know a lot of other servers). Fortunately, the SGC exceeds New York State Minimum Wage laws! The raise in hourly pay more than pays for my gas and tolls to Niagara Falls. The number '$8,400 in fringe benefits is just a figure on a page, until you break it down.

On 'Day 1' of my employment (my training was at $8/hour; ask a server/bartender you know what they were paid for 'training' at your local restaurant/bar); I was paid to sit and become educated on the many benefits the SGC extends to its employees. Such as: free meals and, I'm paid while I'm eating the free meal! Yes, for an 8-hour shift, I'm entitled to a 30-minute meal break, and two 15-minute breaks, but I'm paid for the entire 8 hours. NYS law requires employers to allow a 30-minute break in a 6-hour period – but, the employer may deduct this 30-minute break from the employee's pay. Yeah, I guess it's just another example of how the SGC 'ignores' NYS labor laws.

What else? I have 7 paid Holidays! And, if I work the Holiday? I get paid double-time; for all you servers toiling on holidays at minimum wage, my pay computes to $10.50 per hour, plus tips. On November 7, 2006, I'll have 2 weeks' paid vacation (For servers? Are you kidding me?) And guess what? This past Christmas (a Sunday, the last day of my work week), the last few hours were also overtime (Federal labor laws DO apply on Nation land). So, I was making double-time-and-a-half. I have never before made 2-1/2 times my base pay, plus tips, for waiting on tables.

And what else? Well, Mr. Jackson, I get one sick day per month for EVERY MONTH that I work for them – and can even sell them back at the end of the year! Didn't get ANY of that on Elmwood Avenue or Franklin Street. And, here's the kicker. The where-do-I sign-on-the dotted-line-because-this-is-too-good-to-be-true-benefit: after 3 full months of employment, on the same day my other benefits kicked in, I became eligible for the Seneca Gaming Corporation's 401(k) Plan, with a 50% employer matching funds contribution, up to 1.5% of my annual pay. Tell that to your server tonight when you are dining out.

Don't talk to me about the low-pay and no benefits. I have the facts. I can tell that for the 6 weeks that followed Thanksgiving week, I made 10% more waiting tables at the Casino than I did last year during the same period. And, the SGC gave me a turkey to boot! Then, in my 6th week, I received a $100 Holiday Bonus from the casino. Haven't ever received a turkey or a Holiday Bonus while working at Buffalo-area restaurants. I'd be happy to sit down with you and bring all of my records of the last 6+ years of waiting on tables and present you with the facts as outlined above.

A Lawyer's Perspective

Let me review Bruce Jackson's 'interview' with Dianne Bennett in *Artvoice* (v5, n4, January 26, 2006). First, another disclosure: From September 1984 until November, 1998, I had my own businesses based in Buffalo, and my attorney of record was Hodgson, Russ, Andrews, Woods & Goodyear. Ms. Bennett recently retired from Hodgson Russ, where she was president. I never had any dealings with Ms. Bennett on any legal matters, and, in fact, never met her until the last few years when I began waiting on tables in restaurants. Always a gracious lady to serve. Now on to the 'interview'.

Ms. Bennett makes the point that casinos on sovereign land, "(do not have to play by our rules that (do) not have the protections that we've built up over the years" and calls into question why we would "trust you guys to have a decent workplace." She asks, "Why should they?" How about because it's the right thing to do, and the SGC figured this out a while back, without having to be dragged into litigation? I realize she's an attorney, but not every corporation is out to 'do the minimum, or less'. As I already mentioned, the SGC exceeds many of NYS's labor laws (such as paying better than minimum wage!). And, I-m thankful for this fact, because the benefit of ignoring a 'minimum'. By going beyond it, accrues to me, and my co-workers.

I'm not Living in a Black Hole

How about another 'Big, Bold Lie'? Back to one of Mr. Jackson's articles in *Artvoice* (v5, n3, January 19, 2006). He states, "The money you spend in a (non-casino) restaurant pays for the restaurant's physical plant, its supplies and utilities, and its employees. If the suppliers and utility providers and workers are within the community, they in turn spend the money they get from that restaurant, and that spending provides more jobs and more taxes." He then contrasts this with spending in a casino and states, "It is money that doesn't stay around, that leaves the community as soon as it is spent." Oh really? What about me? What about my co-workers? What about the 'suppliers and utility providers' to the casino? We don't live in a 'black hole', nor do we live in a vacuum. We spend our money in the community just like everybody else does. How can Mr. Jackson make such blatantly false statements and pass them off as facts? Why does he continuously ignore published, verifiable facts? You want to verify this? Then meet with me! I'll bring you the facts. That 401(k) I mentioned? I now have, just since March 1, 2006, over $2,170 in my 401(k). That's over $2,170 more in 401(k) savings than I've had at any point waiting on tables in the past 6 years in Buffalo.

Yes, some Businesses will Close Next Year

In another *Artvoice* article (v5, n8, 'There Goes the Neighborhood'), Mr. Jackson mentions a few businesses that have gone bust, or are about to, since the Seneca Niagara Casino opened. Somehow, in Mr. Jackson's reasoning, this is all the fault of the casino. Guess what? Several bars and restaurants closed in Buffalo over the past year. Some were new businesses and some were long-established businesses. And the Seneca Buffalo Creek Casino has yet to draw one patron spending one dime! Year in and year out, businesses of all stripes open, and businesses of stripes close. It's the way it goes. In every city in America, nay, around the world, this happens. And this will continue to happen in Buffalo – next year, and the year after that, and the year after that. With or without a casino, this WILL happen.

I find it a little one-sided to mention only those businesses that have not fared too well in Niagara Falls, and then to 'across-the-board' lay the blame at the feet of Seneca Gaming Corporation. What about the Holiday Inn Select in Niagara Falls? Why did you fail to mention that this was recently purchased by InterContinental Hotels Group for several million dollars, and is undergoing a major renovation (in the millions of dollars)? If you go to their website, you'll find the first 'major tourist attraction' they mention that is in close proximity to their property is the Seneca Niagara Casino. Heck, they're across the street from the casino! And yet they're investing millions of dollars? Why? Perhaps they know something that Mr. Jackson and others do not.

Another (ongoing) development in downtown Niagara Falls is Carl Paladino's major renovation and conversion of the United Office Building. Oh, right, Mr. Jackson doesn't appear to be a big fan of Mr. Paladino, nor (apparently) anything that he does. However, this doesn't negate the fact that he's pouring a lot of money into downtown Niagara Falls. And, for the record, I recently asked Mr. Paladino, point blank, if he would be doing this project if the Seneca Niagara Casino was not in existence. His one word answer: "No." And, he gave me permission to quote him on this.

Sorry that, once again, the facts don't always support Mr. Jackson's arguments. Terribly inconvenient.

## The Demolition of the H-O Oats Grain Elevators

Another big issue I had with Mr. Jackson was his article (*Artvoice*, v5n23, 'Greed') concerning the demolition of the H-O Oats grain elevators. I attended the ground-breaking ceremony in Buffalo in December, 2005. I viewed the decaying buildings slated for demolition. I am all for historic preservation. I saw little of value in the H-O Oats grain elevators. Those buildings were vacant for years, and few seemed to care what an eyesore they truly were. There are plenty of other grain elevators than can be saved in Buffalo. More than enough. For what purpose, I'm not sure.

I won't rehash all the rhetoric, but, once again, it was 'Much Ado About Nothing'. I'm NOT saying that the dust (yeah, the non-toxic, albeit annoying, dust) wasn't a pain to those living nearby. But, I happen to have friends who lived in 3 separate units of the 'The Lofts at Elk Terminal', and they were very pleased with the weekly vehicle washing and apartment cleaning that the SGC provided to them. And, if Mr. Jackson was so concerned with Asbestos in the air, why on earth did he keep going back and getting coated in that dust? We've all read the EPA conclusions on this matter. Not toxic. Annoying, but not toxic.

The H-O Oats grain elevators are now history. All that's left is to continuously rehash an argument that was not worth having in the first place. What historical value? I say, 'none'. What toxic, asbestos-laden dust? It appears, according to the EPA, 'None'. Enough!

One more thing I'd like to point out here though. The Seneca Gaming Corporation is not in the building demolition business, so they hired professionals to do it for them. Why is it so difficult to wrap your mind around this process? You hire a professional to do something that you, yourself, cannot do. You enter into a contract. You stipulate who is responsible for what. And when there is a SNAFU, the responsible party gets called to task. Who did the EPA fine? Oh yeah, I remember reading they fined the demolition contractors.

Another point on this particular article? I found it interesting that in the June 29, 2006 issue of *Artvoice* (v5, n26), in the 'Letter to *Artvoice*' section, there was 'A Class Discussion' by seventh-grade students at the Oracle Charter School on Delaware Avenue. These seventh-grade students (12- and -13-year olds) studied and commented on Mr. Jackson's 'Greed' article.

They came across as very articulate, and they could 'read between the lines' and 'around the rhetoric' rather well for being in the seventh-grade. They discussed Native rights. They questioned Mr. Jackson's "exaggerating and using swear words to try to offend and scare people." Well said, young people!

Mr. Jackson, I can cuss with the best of 'em. In fact, I have a rather foul mouth and it has often led to troubles. But, I keep this under control when writing in a public forum. It seems appropriate to do so. What's with all the 'F@#* You' and 'F@#* Off' coming from you? FYI, I don't think it serves your purpose. It just sounds like a lot of street-language coming from a 60-something-year-old man.

At this point, I'd like to thank *Artvoice* for continuing to publish letters that disagree with Mr. Jackson. While there hasn't been much in the way of presenting another angle to this story (until here and now), the letters at least attempt to refute some of Mr. Jackson's articles.

Atlantic City: Boom or Bust?

Now, how about that Atlantic City, NJ situation? Over and over, from Mr. Jackson and others, I hear what a mess that city is after many years of casino gambling. This summer, many of us read about the debacle concerning New Jersey's failure to pass a budget, resulting in the closing of many government agencies, including the state auditors who work at casinos.

One of the articles I read (*The Buffalo News*, Thursday, July 6, 2006) was by John Curran of the Associated Press, and was titled 'State budget woes leave Atlantic City casinos eerily quiet'. In the article, Mr. Curran states, "The calm was in stark contrast to the usual scene in this vibrant, open-all-night city, which was rescued from oblivion in the 1970s when city fathers turned to casino gambling in a last-ditch effort to revive the place...", and, "Since the first casino opened ...", there are now" ...a dozen casinos employing 46,000 people." And further, "...fueling the growth of hundreds of small business"

I'm confused. So, which is it? A city in decline or a 'vibrant, open-all-night city'? I'm not, nor is anyone else to my knowledge, proposing a dozen casinos in downtown Buffalo. But can you understand what I'm saying? He says 'this' and she says 'that'. Where does the truth lie? Usually somewhere in the middle.

Tying in Other Issues

I am not saying I'm qualified to look into the future and say with any certainty whether Seneca Buffalo Creek Casino will be good or bad for Buffalo. But, based on my experience, limited though it may be, I have no fears.

Why am I not alarmed with the coming Buffalo Seneca Creek Casino, as Mr. Jackson apparently is? Well, aside from all the items I enumerated above (and can back up with 6-1/2 years of detailed records), I also have experience with the Buffalo and Fort Erie Public Bridge Authority, which Mr. Jackson continuously ties into this issue. I was a customs brokers at the Peace Bridge from 1984 to 1998. I was in the original meetings that the Authority organized in the late 1980s, wherein the (then) Director of Bridge Operations (his name escapes me as it was long ago) outlined the need for bridge expansion. He stated, without hesitation, that building a new bridge was simply not an option, "would cost a billion dollars". This is WAY before 'Twin Span' and 'Signature Span'. And look where we're at on that issue.

Jobs for the Cobblestone District

Much has been written about locating Seneca Buffalo Creek Casino in the Cobblestone District, and some have accused the Seneca Gaming Corporation of 'preying' on the many poor who live there. What about jobs? Isn't this an excellent opportunity for people who LIVE in the Cobblestone District to now have the possibility to WORK in the Cobblestone District? Who else is 'coming to town' with a 1000+ jobs in this area?

Won't many of these local residents apply for the many different jobs being created? Surely there are many people who need a job, want a job and will apply for a job. Like the rest of us, if they're qualified they only need to pass a drug test. Transportation would be a non-issue for the locals. Many could literally walk to work.

And working for the Casino would solve the 'big issue' that seems to concern those who state/imply that SGC is 'preying' on the locals. That is, once you work for Seneca Gaming Corporation, you cannot gamble in any of their facilities. Kill two birds with one stone, you see?

In addition to the pay and benefits they will receive, as an employee of Seneca Gaming Corporation, they may bring up to five people to any Seneca property and enjoy a meal in one of the many restaurants, and receive the 25% Employee Discount on the food bill. Just another add-on bonus we enjoy.

**The Smoking Issue**

When Seneca Niagara Casino opened on December 31, 2002, smoking in the Casino was permitted. In fact, smoking was still permitted in much of New York State. In restaurants, bars, etc., albeit with some restrictions. The following summer (2003), NYS implemented a change in the law that, basically, eliminated smoking in public places. The Seneca Gaming Corporation did not change their laws/rules, but continued to allow what NYS had, until then, allowed for years and years.

Suddenly, Indian-owned casinos are the bad guys. I'm not getting this. This is still America, right? Having an advantage is the name of the game. Just ask a couple of bar/restaurant owners on the NYS border with another state that permits smoking (and most do, by the way); one owner in NYS, one owner in a bordering state. Do you think that the owner in the bordering state would change the rules in his bar to reflect NYS law, or is he going to enjoy his advantage? Exactly.

'You are not protected by NYS Labor Laws'

Telling me that, as an employee of a sovereign nation, I am not protected by NYS Labor laws may be technically true. Just the same as a New Yorker working across the state line in, say, Pennsylvania is not protected by NYS Labor laws. However, I DO have protection on the other side of the NYS line, whether I am working in Pennsylvania or, as in my case, at a Seneca Gaming Corporation property.

The SGC has some of the most stringently-enforced policies I have seen working in the hospitality industry. They take issues of discrimination and workplace harassment quite seriously, and I have personally witnessed employee termination when one does not adhere to policy. I feel more protected than at any time in the past 6-1/2 years.

Summing it Up: Bring it on!

No, I say the sky is not falling. Buffalo is not going to go down the drain when the Seneca Buffalo Creek Casino opens. Some minimum-wage with zero-paid-benefits server and bartender jobs will be lost, as businesses close every year. But now they can be replaced with above minimum-wage, full-benefits positions. Bring it on – I hope to see you there myself.

Now that I'm somewhat over the initial anger I felt with the whole 'whorehouse' comment, allow me to (with tongue-in-cheek) point out another flaw in Mr. Jackson's argument. Based on all the above, if the Senecas were to, in fact, open a whorehouse, no doubt they'd be good-paying jobs with full benefits. All that and the Seneca's would be collecting some decent income taxes on behalf of the State & Federal governments!

In closing, let me make one final observation. What is with all talk about the casinos being tax-exempt? It's a fact, and Mr. Jackson even admits it, that the State of New York gets 25% of the revenues from the casinos' slot operations. That's 25% of revenue, NOT 25% of profit. What other industry pays the state (any state) 25% of their revenue? It might not be called a 'tax' per se, but it sure seems like one helluva tax burden to me!

I could continue on refuting so much more that has been written, and maybe I will at some point in the future (just last month I received the current issue of 'Going Places', published by AAA of Western and Central New York; the cover story was 'The Hottest Travel Spot in the West!", and you guessed it, it was about Las Vegas), but for now, I think readers have been given enough to consider from the other side of this ongoing discussion.

Lastly, yes, I do have fears about writing an article for publication in a public forum. What will my employer say (and, while Mr. Jackson will likely dispute the fact, the Seneca Gaming Corporation did not authorize or contribute to my article)? What will my co-workers have to say -"sucking up to the 'man'?" Whatever. I wrote this because I chose to. Period.

And, before anyone can say this was written 'by' the SGC or a Member of the SNI, let me make a proposal. I would be happy to submit to polygraph, and you may ask me:

1) Do you really believe everything you wrote? 'Absolutely', and

2) Did anyone from the Seneca Gaming Corporation and/or any Member of the Seneca Nation of Indians contribute, in any way, to this article? 'Absolutely not'.

Then, I would like to have the same opportunity to question Mr. Jackson and other *Artvoice* contributors.

1) Have you published, and do you continue to publish, statements/facts/statistics that you know to be false and/

or misleading in the hopes of bolstering your argument against a Buffalo casino?

Note: The temporary Seneca Buffalo Creek Casino opened July 3, 2007. The SNI opened their 9 million expansion of the temporary casino in early 2010. There are slot machines only at the Buffalo Creek Casino.

Also note, that wages quoted in Hal's article, have since increased based on annual wage increases in the industry.

**WHO KNEW WHERE EDUCATION WOULD TAKE HIM**

The publication of Hal's article and the reader responses led directly to the extension of Hal's education. Hal began classes at Erie Community College in the Fall of 2007 with the encouragement of Harriet H. Fox, now an 89-yearold friend he met at the Western Door Steakhouse in 2006. Harriet said, "He wanted to go to school, but wanted someone to go with him because he didn't want to be the oldest kid in the class." From that meeting, a whole new venture began.

Hal and Harriet started classes together on September 10, 2007, her 86th birthday. In May, 2010, Hal had the honor of presenting her with a 'Lifetime Learning Award' bestowed upon her from Phi Theta Kappa International Honor Society, of which Hal became, a member in the spring of '09.

Hal completed his Associates Degree in Liberal Arts – Humanities/Social Science in August, 2010. He has also taken Spanish Courses (summer school 2010 and 2011).

As a transfer student, Hal began classes at State University of New York at Buffalo (UB), in the fall of 2010 (English Major), and plans to complete his Baccalaureate Degree in the spring of 2012. He then hopes to begin the Law Degree Program at the University of Buffalo in the Fall of 2012. His plans include the study of Native American Treaty Law/ Casino Law (and relevant Constitutional Law). Upon completion of his studies, Hal would like to remain an employee with the Seneca Gaming Corporation and hopefully move

into their Law Department at the appropriate time......
all going back to his published article 'Jackpot: A Casino
Employee Speaks Up (And Trumps all Those Little White
Lies & Big Bold Lies)'. (See: http://archives.buffalorising.
com/entries/print article/buffalo_casino_the flipside_0).

**Casino Contribution:** The Casino has assisted Hal with his educational endeavors by providing financial reimbursement for partial tuition and books (if work related). As well, Hal has full support from his Supervisor and Department Head, and has always enjoyed a flexible work schedule which enables him to attend school full-time while also working full-time (evening hours).

I wonder where his education will take him. I think Hal should be writing a book on his educational journey and his life experiences to date. He really is a remarkable person. This is such an inspirational story and I am so pleased that I met this most interesting, and industrious mature student. Another Winner!

**Update:** As of September, 2011, Hal has successfully completed his Spanish courses, and is still working full-time evenings at Seneca Niagara (Western Door); he is attending the University of Buffalo as a full-time student and diligently studying to accomplish his educational and career goals. Good Luck Hal.

Note: I chose to include Hal's story because of his commitment to his job and the importance of setting straight the facts presented by the media based on his own employment in the industry.

**SOME PEOPLE MAKE THE WORLD SPECIAL JUST BY BEING IN IT!**

♣ ♦ ♥ ♠

# CHAPTER 5
# CASINO ETIQUETTE

**CASINO ETIQUETTE (SOMEONE HAS TO TELL THEM!)**

How many times have you sat down beside someone or they have sat down beside you and you detected an unpleasant odor? Whether it be at the movies or at any public gathering, body odor is not pleasant. Neither is it healthy to have someone with a cold or other ailment that could be contagious, sitting beside you at a slot machine or table game. If you are not well, please stay home and get well.

**YOU CAN SEE HOW IMPORTANT MANNERS ARE BY WATCHING PEOPLE WHO DON'T HAVE ANY**

Be considerate:

1. Please be clean and try to use deodorant when visiting the casino; at least shower or bathe.

2. Please do not bring your cold or virus with you.

3. Try to dress appropriately; short shorts on big men or women are not very appealing, especially if the weather outside is freezing. Remember, casinos are usually kept very cool. Too-low tops on women can be distracting to dealers; some cleavage may be attractive but in many cases is not.

Please do not wear T-shirts with profanity written on them. I personally do not think that Casinos should allow this type of offensive attire.

4. When at the tables, please refrain from using profane language or blaming dealers for a bad hand. They deal the cards not select them for you.

5. When at the slot machines, please do not bang, pound or hit the machine. If you are losing, try moving on to other machines or perhaps consider going home. The same applies at the tables; hitting or slamming a table will not help you win. It is Luck. If this is not your lucky day, think about leaving.

6. *If you are a smoker at a table, blow your smoke upwards and not in the face of the dealer or in the faces of other players. I personally do not think that cigar-smokers or any smoking should be allowed at the tables.

If smoking at a slot machine, please use the ashtrays provided and do not deposit your butts in the money/ticket containers.

If smoking at a slot machine, be aware of where and how you are holding your cigarette; players beside you do not need your smoke.

*Smoking is not allowed in Canadian Casinos.

Note: I cannot believe the number of people who are on oxygen and visit casinos where smoking is allowed.

7. Ladies – please do not overdue the perfume.

8. When playing at a table, please do not constantly play with your chips; it is annoying to other players.

9. Ladies – please refrain from carrying big purses; especially at the tables. There is nothing worse than a woman's big purse.

10. When using the washrooms, please throw your garbage in the proper containers provided.

Note: When Casino Rama, Orillia, Ontario, first opened, Casino outdoor maintenance personnel discovered discarded or soiled diapers in the Parking Lots. Containers were placed in the Parking Lots to address this distasteful habit.

11. Deposit all needle paraphernalia in the containers provided (diabetic needles/other).

**Note:** I have mentioned the extremes of bad manners; I must say that Casino washrooms and the gaming environment is kept very clean and are maintained to a high standard set by Casino management.

Gambling is not a spectator sport! Do not stand behind slot players or table players for a long period time of time (unless they don't mind). The people gambling are paying to gamble not to amuse a spectator.

**Note:** I saw a man sitting at a $100 slot machine wearing a T-Shirt on which was written "Gambling Is Not a Spectator's Sport!"

## HE WHO FINDS NO FAULT IN HIMSELF NEEDS A SECOND OPINION

### House Rules

1. When playing at the tables, turn cell phones off; the making or taking calls is not allowed.

2. When playing Blackjack: if you wish to take a card, signal with your finger for an additional card. If you do not want a card, wave off with your hand to make it clear to the dealer that you do not wish a card. The cameras above need to see these hand signals.

3. When playing 3-Card Poker, Caribbean Stud or other table games, keep your cards down in front of you; do not hold your cards up high on your chest and make sure they are over the table ledge, not behind the ledge.

4. Do not discuss or show your hand to other players. If you have a question, ask the dealer or a Floor Boss.

5. Remain seated when playing a table game.

♣ ♦ ♥ ♠

# CHAPTER 6
# CASINO ANTICS

**EXPERIENCES IN THE CASINOS**

**AUG. /2009**

**CASINO ANTICS**

**THE BLIND SIDE**

While sitting at a 3-card Poker table, I soon realized that a *blind man is playing at the table. He was sitting in the fifth player spot. No one was allowed to help him play his hand except the dealer. She dealt the cards and in this game the players are allowed to look at their cards after the deal. After the 'sighted' players decided to stay or fold, the dealer then looked at the blind man's cards and advised him of the cards he was holding. He decides whether he will fold or stay. He must put in his own chips and other players cannot touch his money. The stack of playing chips in front of him kept falling over in the process of making his bet and he then would restack them. This intriguing betting procedure continued and for the time being, all went well at the table. When this man decided to light up a cigarette, this, of course resulted in his maneuvering of the ashtray, ashes in and around the ashtray (as he cannot see the ashtray) the stacking of chips ritual, and the situation soon changed.

**SPARKS FLY**

A lady joined the table and sat in to play the fourth player spot. She had not realized yet that the man beside her is blind. She too is a smoker. Now the fun began. They would be sharing the ashtray. She lit up a cigarette and when she went to put her cigarette in the ashtray, so did the blind man. He burned her finger, she yelped and screamed "oh, you just burned me"; he jumped around and said "I am so sorry, I didn't see you!" She was speechless. The table broke up laughing. What can I say; it was a casino moment. You had to be there.

*I found out later that this gentleman was known as a 'regular' and a friend brought him to the casino, got him settled at a table, would come back to get him and drive him home.

## STUPID IS AS STUPID DOES

A man in his 40s with an older woman (both had been drinking), sat down at the table where I was playing Blackjack. The man had a T-shirt on that had an inscription on the front which read: Do I Look Fucking Stupid?

A male floor boss was at my right-elbow and I quietly asked him if a player could be asked to leave a table or put on a jacket to cover an obscene T-shirt. He glanced at the shirt and then smirked and whispered to me "Not Really." I thought that was a poor answer, and also wondered why a female player or for that matter, any player, including the dealer, should have to look at an obscene T-shirt? Just then another young female player joined the table and sat beside him. We continued to play. The dealer dealt a hand and the 'obscene guy' got a pair of Kings. The dealer had a 6-up-card. The guy split the Kings and all players at the table were not amused. We all lost the hand, including him. The younger girl said, "Why did you split the Kings"? He replied, "That's none of your fucking business." The floor boss then came over to the table and cautioned the player that 'bad language' is not tolerated. I thought to myself: not only "Do you Look F------ Stupid, you are F------ Stupid. He didn't stay long and we sure didn't miss him.

Shortly after this episode, a female floor boss relieved the male floor boss. I quietly asked her why obscene wording on T-shirts was allowed at the gaming tables. She looked at me and responded, "Oh, I have never been asked that question" and I never did get an answer.

Incidentally, this was the only unpleasant situation I had ever experienced in a casino. The Floor Bosses and security watch for the inebriated patron or unruly people in the Casino, and as a rule, most people are friendly and display proper table etiquette.

**THE HAIRY SIDE**

On one occasion, while sitting at a Caribbean Stud table, a very large man who was handicapped and sitting in a very big custom-designed, motorized wheelchair, was playing at the table. He was in the end spot and was accommodated by staff who removed two end player chairs to enable him to position himself to play. I was sitting to his right. I soon realized that this man was not entirely comfortable in his upright position. At one point, when I looked to my left, I was staring at a huge hairy belly! Oh my, where to look, where to look. Why was he now in a horizontal position? Because of his obvious discomfort, he would put his wheelchair in the reclining position to make himself more comfortable. This resulted in his shirt rising up to expose his big hairy belly. This happened many times between the dealing of hands. I just kept my eyes forward; I continued playing as I was winning! To say the least, this was a rather 'hairy experience'.

**THE 'BUNGEE CORD'**

On one occasion, when Carole (another dear friend of mine; now deceased) and I were at the Fallsview Casino, she got up from her seat and walked away from a slot machine but had forgotten to remove her Player's Card. While walking away, the cord got caught on a man who was sitting and playing at a machine. She was not aware that it was wrapped around the poor man and continued on her way until she heard "Whoa, Whoa, Lady, You're strangling me!" Horrified, she quickly stopped, rushed back, and untangled her cord from the man's neck, apologized profusely and then all the people who had seen this 'bungee cord tango' broke up laughing. "Turn me loose!"

Note: It is not uncommon for players to leave or lose their Player's Card at the Casino. All one has to do is go to the Customer Service /Players Advantage/Promotion counters, and it will be replaced.

While the Bungee Cords are free in Canadian and most U.S. Casinos, one must buy them at the Gift Shop in some Casinos in Las Vegas (usually US$1.00).

Tip: I found that the 'Bungee Cord' makes for a great patio umbrella-wrap cord.

### A RIDE WITH AN APE

One day Carole and I took the Casino bus to the Niagara Casino (now known as the old Casino). On this particular occasion, the Casino had a jungle theme going on. When we entered the Casino, there were huge people-size stuffed animals hanging from the balconies, ceilings, and other areas throughout the Casino. Players were eligible to win these animals, and I recall commenting to Carole "Imagine winning one of those things, where would you put it?"

When Carole and I went to the Casino, we would split up when we arrived and arrange to meet for a coffee, split again, and then meet at the boarding area for the bus trip home. Well, you can imagine my surprise when we met to go home. Carole was standing in line, struggling with this huge orangutan that was taller than she. We named our new travelling companion Big Bill. When we got on the full bus, there was no place to sit Big Bill. The whole bus was laughing and finally, with the help of the bus driver, we put him in the Washroom at the back of the bus.

Carole told me that when she arrived home, she placed Big Bill inside the door of the front entrance of their townhouse, and when Bill, her husband, came in the door, it scared him half out of his wits.

### SIDE BAR

As mentioned before, drinks are free at the U.S. casinos and, of course, some patrons tend to take advantage of this perk. I have never seen anyone too inebriated, and if they are, they will be asked to leave.

Once, when I sat at a table in the Smoking section (the non-smoking section did not have a Caribbean Stud table and that is why I was in this section), a one young woman sitting on an end spot, looked like she had already had a few drinks. You are allowed to have one drink, at a time, at the tables. Actually there is no more room for any more, as with the seating capacity (7 players at a table) and with the curve and shape of the table, there just isn't enough space. If it is a Smoking table, the table must accommodate the ashtray/s as well. Anyway, this young lady ordered another drink, proceeded to knock it over, and it spilled onto the ashtray, cards, and the table. This was when the table was shutdown, the players were asked to leave, and of course, the mess had to be cleaned up, table dried, the cards destroyed, and the dealer is now without his/her table. Of course, the young woman was embarrassed and when she hurriedly got up, she dropped her purse, the contents fell out and now there is a 'floor scramble' to pick up her assortment of things. She muttered as she left "I hate this purse!"

I have always said "There is nothing worse than a woman's purse"; especially at a gaming table.

I was a bit disappointed that this table was closed down, as I had just played a few hands and was winning.

**ACCEPT THAT SOME DAYS YOUR'RE THE PIGEON, AND SOMEDAYS YOU'RE THE STATUE**

**CARD COUNTER**

In January, 2010, I interviewed 45-year old Mike, who lived in Las Vegas for 7 years and told me his story.

Mike usually played table games, sports betting and video poker. When playing Blackjack, he would keep track of the cards. He said, "It was easier to do when the cards were dealt by a dealer. It is more difficult to do now because of the Automatic Card Shufflers and the extra decks added, e.g., 4, 5, 6 or 8 decks of cards." The most he won in one night was $7500 betting at a $25 table. The longest he has played was for a 16-hour stint. He has been asked to leave the Blackjack table in a number of Las Vegas casinos. Some 'counters' or players are advised not to come back to a casino, although that hasn't happened to Mike. When you are on 'the list' you cannot enter their casino.

He did say that Las Vegas was suffering because of the rapidly expanding casino industry in Canada and the U.S., and Real Estate had fallen by almost 50%. The drop in housing prices did help the people who stayed in Las Vegas; about 300 housing auctions were being held weekly while he was there and he said there were some great housing bargains to be had. As well, the remaining people were appealing their taxes based on the decreased property values.

Commercial property sales were down 70% affecting the Legal profession, Education (enrollment in the schools) and many projects in the construction industry were halted or did not go forward because of the downturn in the global economy, which of course, affected Las Vegas. With an approximate 10% drop in Employment and the ripple effect on other areas of employment, this resulted in over a 20% drop in the Las Vegas economy.

Fact: There is no State Income Tax in Las Vegas.

One interesting point: When people walked away from their homes, as some did, many did not bother to drain their swimming pools. This became a problem because the combination of stagnant water and the intense Las Vegas heat resulted in many mosquitoes which created a West Nile Virus problem.

A big concern for Las Vegas is the drain and use of power. On our last visit, when flying into Las Vegas, I could not believe how the water level of Lake Mead had receded; at one time it was a huge lake.

Mike an Accountant, helped expose the fraud at Philip Services Corporation in Hamilton, Ontario (1996-97). That is a whole different story that is still in the courts.

♣ ♦ ♥ ♠

## CHAPTER 7
## THE PROMOTIONS/PERKS

## THE PROMOTIONS/PERKS

### The Player's Card

When you visit any casino, you are encouraged to apply for a Player's Card. This involves presenting valid government-issued photo identification (a Driver's License, Passport or Health Card). The age for gambling is 21 in the US (or wherever alcohol is served).

You receive a Player's Card which has your name and an assigned number on it. It is usually attached to a 'bungee cord' to hook onto your purse, belt, around the neck, etc.

### Points Equals Status

Using the Player's Card when playing the slot machines, or presenting it at a table game/s, accumulates points for the player, e.g., for every $20 spent in a slot machine, a point is earned (sometimes double points are awarded); points earned at table games are based on the table bet ($5/$10/$25 or higher), the buy-in chip amount, and how long you play at the table/s. A player can use these points toward meals, gifts, and show tickets or for other promotions offered on a regular basis by the casino/s. The more money wagered, the more points accumulated, which takes you to another level of play or eligibility for promotion status, e.g., the Chairman's Club.

Once on the player/promotion list, you begin to receive a monthly newsletter with that month's weekly promotion and other information. These promotions include free buffet lunches/dinners/restaurant credits, varying amounts of free slot-play dollars ($5 to $300), tickets for entertainment and/or complimentary rooms, shopping sprees, entries for Sweepstake draws, luxury cars, and vans, entry into Blackjack, 3 Card Poker or 'Texas Hold Em' poker tournaments, and other perks. On certain dates, a player may exchange earned points for double-amount slot play. The promotions are numerous and are mailed out on a regular basis. The Marketing and Promotion people are very creative with the attractive and enticing offers.

The *entertainment/shows are excellent and we have on occasion taken advantage of these shows, e.g., at the Fallsview - Spirit of Christmas, a wonderful show with favorite holiday carols, great cast of singers and dancers and gorgeous costumes. We have seen The Nitty Gritty Dirt Band at Seneca Niagara, and we also attended a fantastic cooking seminar with top Chefs from the Seneca Niagara restaurants.

*The entertainment industry has benefited greatly from the Casinos in that they employ many singers, dancers, comedians, musicians as well as lounge/bar entertainment.

Incidentally, of the many Seneca Niagara promotion offers I have taken advantage of are: a set of luggage, a Lady and Man Watch Set, and a fine all-weather jacket for my son-in-law; these were all top-quality merchandise. The Casino also gives Hams and Turkeys around Thanksgiving and Christmas.

Note: There are time limits and specific dates when the promotions can be used for dollar-amount Free Slot Play, and/or the free gifts to be picked up, and when travel 'junkets' or room offerings can be used.

The Fallsview Casino had an offer of Gift Certificates in denominations from $10, $25 and $100 which could be redeemed at any Fallsview Casino Niagara restaurant, the Box Office for tickets to the entertainment, the Galleria Gift shops or at the Casino Resort's Hotel & Spa.

Promotions can also include invitations to other Casinos in North America, Australia, and the United Kingdom or wherever one has visited/obtained a Player's Card.

If you need additional information regarding a promotion or complimentary offer, you can contact a casino Host or Hostess.

Following is an interview with a Casino Hostess:

**Job Position: Casino Hostess**

**Seneca Niagara Casino**

In October, 2011, I was able to interview Lorraine (not her real name), a Casino Hostess. She has been with Seneca Niagara since it opened in December, 2002.

Her job responsibilities include helping patrons with their individual concerns, booking hotel rooms, event tickets, and assisting with many of the hotel functions. Her main objective is "to provide the best customer service that she can."

Lorraine likes everything about her job; there was nothing about her job that she didn't like. When asked if she would like to advance to any other casino positions, she advised that she was content where she is.

She mentioned that the skills required for this position are: good listening and speaking skills. As well, it is important to be knowledgeable about all the promotions available, in order to assist the clients/patrons with correct information.

As stated before, the type of Player Card that one is eligible for is based on the time and money spent in a given playing area of the casino, e.g., table games/slots. The type of Player's Card held is the determining factor on what comps/perks are awarded to a patron.

Lorraine said she does not gamble but has visited other casinos, e.g., The Fallsview, Fort Erie Slots and the Windsor Casino.

She ended the interview with the comment that Seneca Niagara is a very good employer and is very good to all their employees.

**A JOB WORTH HAVING IS A JOB WORTH SACRIFICING FOR**

♣ ♦ ♥ ♠

## CHAPTER 8
## THE ADVENTURES

# THE ADVENTURES

## MELBOURNE, AUSTRALIA
## FEB. /1999

My long-time friend (for over 50 years) Barbara was going to visit her widowed sister Eileen in Australia. She and Eileen invited me to spend the month of February with them. I had never been away from my husband or daughter for that long of a holiday and was a bit leery about going away for such a long holiday. Len (my husband) was very supportive and said "Go ahead, you have always said that it was one place you wanted to visit and you may not get an opportunity like this again." Kelly and her husband Steve also encouraged me to go.

What an exciting adventure and experience that was. I had met Eileen many years before as she and Barbara take turns visiting one another back and forth many times. They still do. Eileen was the most wonderful hostess and made me feel so at home. She had a room all set up for me with an empty closet and dresser drawers which really made me feel like a "wanted house guest."

We had so many fabulous outings (her friends were just great and threw some wonderful dinner parties). We went on a great wine tour of the vineyards and sampled some very tasty wine and heard some great jazz bands along the way. We played golf at Eileen's Golf Club in Croydon (a suburb of Melbourne), had High-Tea in a lovely Hotel in Melbourne, a River Cruise and toured in and around Melbourne, and were even there for Barbie's 40$^{th}$ Birthday (that is the Barbie Doll Barbie). A huge statue of Barbie was downtown for the tourists to see and it really was a big hit. Some people are easily amused! Myself included.

We flew to Tasmania, and spent a few days in Hobart (the state capital) where we rented a car and toured the countryside. We stayed at a lovely country Inn, had 'smashing' meals and just had a fabulous time. Tasmania is an Australian island and state of the same name, located 150 miles south of the continent. Hobart was founded in 1804 as a penal colony and is Australia's second oldest capital city after Sydney.

One of the many highlights of this trip was an evening at the Crown Casino in Melbourne. Eileen's boss Ailsa owned and managed her own business and hosted a dinner party for her staff at the Crown Casino. She invited Barbara, Eileen and I as her guests. She also had tickets for us all to see the floorshow "Manpower" (male strippers). Oh my, I really wasn't into male strippers but what the heck – "don't look a gift horse in the mouth" and you never know unless you go! Well, that was one of the best floor shows I have ever seen. These good-looking young gentlemen were marvelous; they appeared in Tuxedos, played various musical instruments, could sing and dance and were extremely talented and just put on a 'magical' professional show. I have never seen such an array of ladies' lingerie (bras and even panties flying through the air and landing on the stage). These gentlemen were gracious, entertaining and never did strip right down; they ended up with their top-hats on, a bow tie and a G-string! Yes, it was quite exciting to say the least. We were 'over the moon'. For the record, I kept my "knickers on."

I didn't have much time to gamble, but did manage to sit down for about a half-hour at a Blackjack table. The most upsetting part of this sojourn was that behind my playing spot on the table, were two more spots, which meant that other players could play those spots and stand behind you. You control the bet, but they are allowed to play the spots. I found this very distracting and I said to the dealer "Sir, do I have to let these people play behind me?" He looked at me and said "Lady, where are you from?" I said "Canada." He laughed and said, "Yes they are allowed to play "piggyback" here. I didn't stay long, as at that time, smoking was allowed in the Casino, and as I do not smoke, I sure didn't appreciate other players standing behind me blowing smoke!

We had a great evening at the Casino and thanked Ailsa for including us in with her Staff Dinner.

Incidentally, Ailsa, Eileen's boss, won $1 million Australian dollars playing the $1.00 slot machines about 8 months before we visited. She of course, is now invited to just about all big events at the Casino. She purchased a Condo in downtown Melbourne and continued running her business.

In Australia they have gaming/slot machines in many locations, and they are called "the Pokies". The pokies/slot machines are official gaming machines and are located in Golf Clubs, pubs and other clubs throughout Australia. We, (Eileen and I) managed to play a few. If I recall, I didn't win a lot nor did I lose a lot. Really, I didn't play that many.

A bit of History:

Australia's population is 20,264,082/one game for every 101 people

Australia has over 20% of the world's gaming machines

There are close to 200,000 machines in Australia

100,308 of these are found in New South Wales

38.6% of adult Australians play the pokies

In 2003/2004, gamblers lost $16.21 billion ($9.1 billion on pokies)

It is estimated that there are over 300,000 problem gamblers

Gambling Facts:

The average player loses $380 every year

The average problem gambler loses $12,000 each year

I will never regret taking the trip to Australia, meeting Eileen's wonderful friends, and visiting the Healsville Sanctuary, seeing Kangaroos, Koala Bears, and we even saw the Tasmanian Devil (in daylight too); what an ugly creature.

The one thing I didn't like: the flight is very long; it took 23 hours going with an hour and a half stopover in Hawaii, on to Sydney for an hour stop, then on to Melbourne, Australia. Coming home, the flight was 25 hours. It took me 9 days to get over the flight; I felt like I was in a tomb and really not quite myself until day 9. I did miss my husband and family and really knew the meaning of 'homesick' (the last week). It is good we were kept busy as there really wasn't that much time to think about it.

Oh yes, after Ailsa won her million, she won another big Jackpot at the Crown Casino; $400,000, and then won another $350,000 – all within 18 months. How is that for luck? What are the odds? Ailsa is now 72 years old and enjoying her retirement immensely.

**TIP:** If you are able and can afford it, take the long trips when you are younger. Do not wait until you are too old, have health problems or just don't want to travel. My parents always said, "We will travel when we are older and retired"; they never did travel (except small jaunts in Ontario or to visit me in Hamilton on occasion), and then they had no desire to travel and were content to stay at home in Kirkland Lake, Ontario.

Note: (Eileen lost her husband Brian when he was 57 years old; Barbara lost her husband, Tony in Dec., 2006). Tony was the best-man at our wedding in 1964).

BIG BEN and LONDON DOUBLE-DECKER BUS

# THE LONDON, UK EXPERIENCE
# MAY/JUNE 2002

## Marnie and I

Marnie and I decided to visit London, England in May/June, 2002. Marnie had visited England several times (about 30 trips over the years, and she and her husband Orv (now deceased) just loved the UK, and Orv had relatives who lived there so they vacationed every chance they got). As I had never been to England and had a former roommate named Jan, now living in Southampton, I thought this was a great opportunity to see London as well as visit Jan.

This was the Golden Jubilee Year and many exciting celebrations were scheduled in London and surrounding areas for the Queen's Golden Jubilee weekend from June 1 – 4.

While driving in from the airport, I noticed a couple of Casino signs. When I inquired about the Casinos, I was told that they were private clubs. How interesting I thought, and wondered if we might have the opportunity to get into one.

We were staying at a lovely hotel in Russell Square called the President Hotel. Our hotel was connected to another hotel that had a shared-lobby area with our hotel and from where you could exit into a small courtyard. We decided to explore the courtyard area and what do you think we see. To the right of this delightful courtyard, which had a lovely water- fountain, was the Gala Casino.

We thought that we would be able to just walk in and look around. That was not to be. We were greeted by a lovely hostess who informed us that in order to visit the Casino, we would have to leave our passports and return in 24 hours to pick up a Player's card upon approval of identification, etc. We did this and were issued an official receipt for our passports for pickup the following day.

The next day, after a full day of touring London and sites, we returned to the Gala Casino to pick up our Passports and Player's cards for entry into the Casino. Marnie decided to go back to the room and I decided to visit the Casino.

One is not allowed to just walk in. I was escorted into the Casino by a hostess and then proceeded to explore. This Casino was much smaller than other Casinos I have visited. The slot machines were on the outer walls and the gaming tables in the middle. I decided to sit at a Blackjack table where the ante was 10 pounds English money. At that time, that amount was worth approximately Cdn. $20. I was totally unfamiliar with the currency at this stage and just sat in to play with my pounds of money.

## BLACKJACK CHAOS

When I sat down, there were five other people at the table. There were two women to the extreme right sitting at the number one and two spots, an Asian lady in the three spot, and now me in the number four spot. Two gentlemen were in the fifth and sixth spots. I won the first hand and the Asian lady lost and was waving her hand around and was upset because she had lost. She just missed my face with her waving hand and I politely asked her not to wave her hand around my face. The second hand I won as well and she lost; this time the lady waved her hand and grazed my face. I called for a Floor Boss and she was then asked to leave. The players and the dealers thanked me. Apparently she had been carrying on before I arrived and the dealer said that a player had to complain before anything could be done; he could not ask her leave. Mind-boggling don't you think?

Too much excitement for me; I played one more hand and then left the table and cashed in. I cashed in approximately Cdn. $60. I thought I could just leave, but quickly discovered that I must be escorted out just as I had been escorted into the Casino. The hostess asked why I was leaving so soon and I advised that we had a busy itinerary planned for the next day. She then asked if a guest and I would be interested in attending the Jubilee Celebration coming up on the Sunday night. Everything was complimentary and I graciously accepted the invitation and off I went.

When I got back to the room Marnie asked how much had I lost. I happily reported that I had won and regaled her with my stressful half-hour sitting at the Blackjack table. We went downstairs to our little bar off the lobby and had a drink to celebrate my win.

## JUBILEE CELEBRATION

What an exciting evening we had at the Jubilee Celebration. Marnie and I thought we were dressed up until we saw the other guests. There were women in beautiful gowns, headdresses, diamonds and bling-bling jewellery. Some men wore tuxedos while others were dressed in robes (from various countries). The room held a great assortment of humanity to say the least. Indeed impressive!

The food was excellent and included caviar, lobster, shrimp, chicken and many other delicacies. The champagne and wine was flowing and the entertainment was superb. There were prizes to be won and a 40-inch TV was the door-prize (we hoped not to win the door prize as it certainly would not fit in return-home luggage).

## LET THE GAMES BEGIN

As Marnie was not a gambler, she chose to sit in the pleasant lounge/bar area, where through a curved glass window she could see into the Casino area. She ordered a glass of wine and was content to listen and see the entertainment and watch a most interesting gathering of people; as well she had an excellent view of the Casino gaming floor.

### Caribbean Stud Win

I decided to sit in at a Caribbean Stud Table. The ante was 15 pounds and there was only one spot available at the table. This is huge for me as I am still not familiar with the currency, but I sit in and hoped for the best.

I notice that there isn't a Progressive Jackpot in this Caribbean Stud game. If there was a Progressive Jackpot, this is where a player/s put up an extra dollar in the circle above each player's spot to be eligible to win a portion of (if you get a Straight Flush) or the whole progressive jackpot amount should you be dealt a Royal Flush. Without the Progressive Jackpot, the payouts were the same as in Canada and the US for winning hands if the dealer opens (with an Ace and King or better) and the player gets paid if you beat the dealer's hand.

The first hand I got was a pair and the dealer opened; I beat the dealer and am paid. The second hand is dealt, and I won that one too with a pair; I then got a flush and was paid five to 1. I am very excited, pick up my chips and leave the table. When I cash in (approximately Cdn. $270), I was asked why I was leaving so soon. I replied that I do not know where I can make this much money in forty-minutes and happily leave.

When I join Marnie, she asks, "Did you lose already?" No, No, says I, "I won." We celebrate and continue to enjoy the rest of the Jubilee Celebration. What an absolutely fabulous free-evening in a London Casino. The winnings helped pay for my shopping in London and I shall never forget that Casino experience and the interesting people we met. A great Jubilee celebration for both of us.

Incidentally, the hostess did tell us that the dealers come from all over the world. I had the opportunity to meet three of them; they were from London, Scandinavia and Italy, and they all said they enjoyed their jobs.

**A JUBILEE STREET SCENE**

While shopping in busy downtown London, a young street musician was sitting on the sidewalk in front of the world-famous *Selfridge Department store. He was playing God Save the Queen on a road cone (a bright orange cone used for blocking off street traffic) and he was very good. What an unusual site and an ingenious young man. I asked if I could take his picture; he happily obliged and I put a pound note in his cap. What a sight and this pleasant patriotic lad just added to another Jubilee moment!

*Selfridge's century-old flagship store is the largest department store on Oxford Street. It is renowned for the innovative displays in its windows, especially at Christmas. One time, one million pounds of diamonds were put on display.

On June 13, 2010, Selfridge's Department store was awarded the "World's Best Department Store," decided on behalf of both the Intercontinental Group of Department Stores (IGDS) and the International Association of Department Stores (IADS).

**UNSETTLING EXPERIENCE**

Marnie and I arrived at the Victoria Train Station in London, where we were catching a train to Southampton to visit Jan (the roommate I had not seen in over 20 years).

While Marnie went to check on what track we would be leaving from, I sat down on a bench to wait. Suddenly a man darted in front of me and asked me to look after his luggage for a minute, and before I had a chance to answer, he took off. Immediately two Security men arrived and quickly asked if that was my luggage, to which I replied "No"; they immediately removed the luggage, put it in a steel-looking container and left. The man did not return. With Security cameras all over the train station, I imagine Security saw something that looked suspicious and moved right in.

We had a great visit with Jan, and she and her friend Carol (now deceased) took us on a day tour and we saw castles, beautiful countryside and even saw a colony of little ponies. We had some fine "Happy Hours" and had a very good lunch and dinner in a couple of the charming English pubs.

While touring London, I mentioned that I wished to visit the London Bridge. Marnie advised that would be impossible as the London Bridge had been moved to Arizona! I was very disappointed as I thought at the time; I will never get to see the London Bridge.

(See the Laughlin, NV Adventure for more on the London Bridge).

**MAY OUR LIFE BE LIKE ARITHMETIC – FRIENDS ADDED, ENEMIES SUBTRACTED, JOYS MULTIPLIED AND TROUBLES DIVIDED**

# THE LAUGHLIN, NV EXPERIENCE
# FEB. /2010

**Marnie and I**

This was another interesting and fun adventure. We were supposed to leave Buffalo/Niagara International Airport at 7:35 p.m. We were delayed and did not get off the ground until 9:00 pm. We had a pleasant flight on a 150-passenger, MD-80 series jet operated by Allegiant Air. We had one stop in Wichita, Kansas to refuel and then flew into Bullhead City Airport in Arizona and arrived at 2:25 a.m. Eastern Time or 11:25 their time.

As soon as we got off the plane there were three big buses waiting to take us to Harrah's Laughlin Casino and Hotel in Nevada. This was a 15-20 minute trip to our hotel. We were greeted by a lovely gentleman who gave us all a string of silver/gold 'lucky beads'. Isn't that marketing at its best!

Into the hotel we went where three tables were set up with registration host/hostesses, and they gave us our information envelope. The envelope provided our Room No. and keys and additional hotel information, e.g., the check-out procedure. We need not worry about our luggage; we do not see it again until it is brought to our room approximately 1-2 hours after we arrive. The room is very nice and an excellent selection of tea and coffee is provided.

Many of the travelers headed right to the Casino. We are very, very weary and could not wait to get to our beds.

**HINT:** Pack your overnight attire in your carry-on if you do not want to wait up for your luggage. You do not have to be concerned about applying for a Player's Card; it too is included in the package. It was a very efficient check-in. They definitely do it all for you. Oh yes, FREE bottles of water were on the tables for us to help ourselves.

**THE PLAYERS**

There are gamblers and there are gamblers. We could not believe how many of the people on this junket knew each other. Marnie pointed out, it is almost like a cult-following; many of the people meet on a regular basis whether it is in Atlantic City, Las Vegas, Mississippi or whenever or wherever the free/low-cost promotions are offered. There were people on this trip from the US but most were from Ontario, Canada.

## A BIT ABOUT LAUGHLIN, NV

What a fascinating little town in Nevada. It is centrally located between the Los Angeles Basin and Phoenix, Arizona, just 90 miles south of Las Vegas. It is set in a rugged mountain terrain which gently slopes to the banks of the Colorado River.

The town was named in 1968 after founder Don Laughlin, owner of the Riverside Resort. Don Laughlin is in his eighties and can usually be found at the Riverside Resort. He is known to pick up paper and debris discarded in and around the casino and apparently is very friendly and accommodating by talking to whomever wishes to chat. Unfortunately, we missed meeting him as he had just left before we got to the Riverside Resort.

A favorite meeting place is the Loser's Lounge at the Riverside and is a popular watering hole for tourists.

Eleven resorts and casinos border on the Colorado River making Laughlin a great adult destination for entertainment and gambling. As well, the casinos provide employment for many of the locals.

The weather is very pleasant during the winter months with day-time temperatures usually mid to upper 60s. During the summer, they rise to the high 90s and 100s. Laughlin is usually 6-10 degrees warmer than Las Vegas because it is south of Las Vegas.

As of this writing, the population of Laughlin is approximately 9,000. The bulk of population and household growth has been attributed to the segment of retirement-age (over 65) and middle-age to near-retirement age (over 45) purchasing homes in the housing market.

Bullhead City, Arizona has a population of approximately 40,000 and as previously stated, is the location of the airport.

No matter where we ventured, the people we met who lived in Laughlin or surrounding areas, or worked inside the casinos or other tourist areas, were absolutely wonderful. They were very helpful, were always smiling and appeared to really enjoy their chosen areas of employment.

I was told that there is a waiting list for employment with Harrah's Casino Hotel. Dealers I spoke with had been there from 5 to 28 years. They stated that Harrah's was a very good employee and they enjoyed their jobs. The age range was from 24 to 65. Much to be said for such a small place in Nevada.

## LAUGHLIN CASINO ENTERTAINMENT

### THE CHROME COWBOYS

The second night in Laughlin I decided to try my luck at the tables. I sat at a Let It Ride $5.00 table where three Texans were playing. There were two brothers and an acquaintance at this table as well as a local player from Bullhead City, Arizona. One brother wore a red shirt and a white Stetson hat while the other brother wore a red/plaid shirt and black Stetson hat. They were very friendly and having many laughs with the dealer. As I said earlier in this book, I love the Texans; the ones I have met are warm, friendly and enjoy themselves. The atmosphere was just great.

I noticed one of the brothers had a beautiful red heart gemstone in front of him and the other brother had a silver key chain with what I thought was an elongated heart or looked like funny 'boobs' on a chain. The other player had a gold nugget shaped as a frog. Most interesting; many players bring various items for luck.

I stayed at this table for two hours as I was winning and also enjoying the company of the players. One of the brothers was losing a bit and I asked the other brother about the elongated heart charm. Is it a heart or 'boobs' I quietly asked him? He broke up laughing and said "Ma'am, to put it proper, they are testicles." Well, the whole table, including the dealer and a floor boss just howled. That truly was a Texas moment. The brothers' wives eventually joined this table as well and they too were fun-loving Texans.

As it was getting late, I wanted to get back to the room by midnight because we were going on a River- Boat Cruise to Havasu City, Arizona, the next morning. When leaving the table, I said goodnight to the Texans and the other players, and told them how much I had enjoyed playing with them. Texan brother Larry, said "Wait Ma'am, I want you to have something and he then presented me with the 'silver balls'. Many laughs again. I did get his business card and found out that this cowboy owns the Cowboy Chrome Shop in Austin, Texas, where they will design, make and ship just about anything world-wide. Check it out on the website: www.CowboyChromeShop.com.

**RIVER ADVENTURE**

We decided to spend a day on the Colorado River. We booked a 6-hr. Jet Riverboat Cruise and arrangements were made to board the boat from the Golden Nugget Dock.

What a pleasant day that turned out to be. We left at 10:00 am and had an excellent 2-hr. narrated boat cruise that took us up the Colorado River to Lake Havasu City, Arizona. We saw million dollar homes overlooking the river as well as small to larger trailer parks. People were fishing on the shores or just parked there to enjoy the beautiful river and scenery. With mountains meeting water and the surrounding scenery and unusual rock formations, this was indeed a wonderful way to spend the day.

The most exciting moment was coming into Lake Havasu and seeing the famous London Bridge. I never thought I would get to see it in Lake Havasu, Arizona.

**THE LONDON BRIDGE**

The London Bridge survived an 1884 terrorist attack and two world wars, and was purchased in April, 1968 from the City of London, England, for US$2.5 million by Robert McCulloch Sr., founder of Lake Havasu City. To avoid taxation, the Bridge was declared an antique and has been identified as the world's largest antique by the Guinness Book of Records.

The Bridge, made up of 2 million pounds of granite (10,276 pieces), was actually dismantled and then shipped from London, through the Panama Canal to Long Beach, CA, and then trucked to Lake Havasu, a 10,000 mile journey. Each brick/stone was numbered and then reassembled like a jig-saw puzzle at a cost of another US$7 million. The lights on the Bridge were constructed from Napoleon's cannons, which had been seized and kept in storage. The cannons were then melted down and forged into lamps for the Bridge. It opened in October, 1971 and now majestically sits as a great tourist attraction. What an undertaking but so worthwhile to enhance this rugged area of Arizona.

A little English Village with English-themed shops, hotels and restaurants line the riverfront at the base of this famous bridge blending the culture of Great Britain with that of the American Southwest.

We docked around 12:15 p.m. at Lake Havasu and had 2 hours to have lunch and explore the quaint little riverfront city.

Lake Havasu is a city in Mohave Country, Arizona. It was founded in 1964 on the shores of Lake Havasu. The present city grew around an old mining town established in the early 20$^{th}$ century. According to the 2006 Census Bureau, the population then was approximately 56,355.

If you ever visit Laughlin, Nevada, this is one outing that is highly recommended and enjoyable. We loved it.

# The London Bridge

Then & Now

## CASINO-HOPPING BY WATER-TAXI

A great way to visit other casinos in Laughlin is by water-taxi. You can buy a one-day ticket for $15.00 (as of this writing) and casino-hop. Each Casino has a dock where the water-taxi passes by every 20-25 minutes for pickups or drop-offs. This is a cheaper way to travel. Otherwise, you may take a cab and pay from $5 to $7 plus tip for each trip from your hotel/casino. Marnie discovered this practical and economical means of transportation and used it to visit the gift shops located in all the river casinos. She had a blast. At one of the shops visited, she purchased three beautiful watches for $19.95 and received the fourth one free. She is still wearing them today (one at a time that is).

We were surprised to learn how many people were not aware of the river water-taxi.

**TIP:** Take a cab if you have a disability or are not prepared for a little walk or climb from the Casino docks. Exception: a couple of the casinos do provide-elevator service from the dock level.

## LEARN TO ENJOY THE LITTLE THINGS – THERE ARE SO MANY OF THEM

## TRIP TO TUNICA, MS
## JAN.FEB./2011

**Marnie and I**

The Limousine picked us up at 1:p.m. and we arrived at Buffalo airport by 1:45 p.m. At 4:15 p.m. we flew out on Allegiant Airlines Jet and arrived in Memphis, TN at 6:00 p.m. their time. The temperature was a pleasant 60 degrees.

We were met by buses and were taken to Tunica, MS where we stayed at the beautiful Verandah Hotel. There is also the Terrace Hotel (where we stayed in August, 2010, and this too is a lovely hotel). Harrah's Casino is separate from the hotels. The Shuttle buses run every 15 minutes from the hotels to the Casino/s. The Harrah's properties are located in Robinsonville and they have three casinos on their property; Harrah's Casino Tunica, Horseshoe Tunica and Hotel, and the Roadhouse (all within 15 to 20 minutes from The Terrace and Verandah hotels). For other recreation options, The Cottonwoods Golf Club and the Tunica National Golf course is nearby as well the Tunica River Park.

When we were in Tunica, MS in August, 2010, I had the pleasure of meeting Mr. Tom L., a casino VIP Coordinator. He gave me his card and I asked if I could send him a hard copy interview regarding his current job and career change. It was through that short meeting that I followed up with a scheduled meeting on this visit.

I called Tom to let him know that we had arrived and we set up the following morning for a phone interview, as that was his day off. Marnie and I had a nightcap at the pleasant little Lobby Bar and then headed to our room for a good night's rest.

The next day it was pouring rain and the temperature had dropped considerably; a very good day for an interview. I called Tom and we had an over-the-phone interview.

**TOM L. – VIP Coordinator**

Tom is 55 years old and has been with Harrah's Tunica Hotel & Casino for a year (at this writing, it will be 3 years). He works with the Marketing Department and Customer Service. Customer service involves providing customers with contacts to the various amenities available at the resorts three self-contained hotels. As well, he handles customer issues as they arise.

Tom, a lawyer, had formerly worked in Boston, MA for 23 years. While attending a conference, he met a lady who owned a Bed & Breakfast in Tunica, MS. They became great friends and to cut a long story short, they got married. He moved to the Tunica area, where he became employed with Harrah's as a VIP Co-coordinator. He enjoys his work; he likes meeting new people and 'the characters and hearing their stories'. On his day's off, he helps his wife with their Bed & Breakfast and really enjoys his new life and career-change for the gaming industry. He said he enjoys this line of work much better than in the legal profession. He did say that employee turnover is high because of the 'burnout' factor.

**YOU WILL NEVER BE SUCCESSFUL AT DOING SOMETHING YOU DON'T WANT TO DO**

## A Little Bit of History

In 1984, Mississippi had the lowest income in the country. When Harrah's opened in 1984, job opportunities and increased revenue for infrastructure had a very positive effect for this small area of Mississippi. Harrah's currently employ approximately 4,000 people in the three casinos/hotel properties.

Harrah's employees have health and wellness benefits, vision and dental care, and an educational assistance program; they also receive discounted memberships at the Public Recreation Centre and Golf courses as well as other amenities. They have employee recognition awards and many of their employees are involved in community charities.

Harrah's have 'responsible gaming ambassadors' on premises and they also offer a day-long gaming program to identify problem gambling.

While speaking with Tom, he suggested that I look up another VIP representative named Mary (not her real name) when I visited Harrah's.

While I took the shuttle bus to Harrah's to spend the morning, Marnie decided to treat herself at the Spa for a Manicure, Pedicure and Hairstyle. (She said it was delightful and she enjoyed her morning immensely).

I shuttled off to Harrah's and located Mary and gave her my business card. I told her that Tom had advised I visit her and perhaps she could show me the "Employee Wall of Fame" (apparently this is a wall of recognition of employees who have contributed to special events in the community and are recognized by the Casino). I was very surprised at the cool reception. She quickly advised that she is not allowed to be involved in any interviews without higher-up approval. I explained that I was only interested in seeing the 'Employee Wall of Fame" which was recommended by Tom. She asked me to come back later and I said I would return if I had time. I chose not to return nor did I get to see the Employee Wall of Fame. I also understood her cool response, as casino personnel must have approval for 'outside interviews'.

While at the Casino, I decided to sit down to play a few hands of Blackjack with a lady dealer. There were no other players at the table, so this gave me the opportunity to chat with her. This turned out to be an interesting meeting. Her name was Margaret and she formerly worked in retail before she was trained as a dealer and now works for Harrah's. She too, loves her job, she does not gamble, but did say she and many other locals were grateful to have their casino jobs (the few dealers I had the opportunity to speak with did not gamble as well).

I played Blackjack for an hour (won $70) and then moved on to another table game I had never played before called Flop Poker. This was a very interesting game where one can play three spots. One spot is for the best poker hand (you use your three cards and two of the dealer's cards) for the best hand, and two other spots (one spot for the ante and the second spot if you think you have a good hand and stay); (you must put up another $5.00 for each spot you play); you should always stay with a pair or better. If you have the best hand of all the players, you get paid on both spots and win the pot. This was a $5.00 table and was a lot of fun. I ended up winning $80, and met some very nice people vacationing from other areas of the U.S.

Before I left the table, I asked a Floor Supervisor if I was eligible for a 'comp' (it never hurts to ask for a comp). She was very pleasant and said she would check. She checked and then advised that she would send a $75 'comp' for me for the Steakhouse. That was a very generous 'comp' and of course, I thanked her.

**A Side Dish/The Other Side**

Before I left to go back to the Hotel, I sat down at a slot machine to try my luck. When I sat down I noticed a very attractive black girl with blonde hair sitting two seats away from me; she looked like she might be in her late 20s/30. I was slowly hitting my buttons at my slot machine (I was taking my time as the money lasts longer) and she was rapidly hitting her buttons). Then I noticed that she was pulling out $20 bills from her rather large bosom. She turned to me and said "This is where I stash my money." Not knowing what to say, I quickly asked her if she lived in Tunica. She said, "Oh no honey, I'm here for the convention." I then said, "Are you having any luck" and she replied, "Oh no hon, I'm losing in here but make the big money outside; I'm a hooker and am just taking a break!" I was so surprised at her answer, I just about fell off my chair. I wished her luck and quickly left. It was shortly after, that I remembered seeing a huge field filled with recreational vehicles, trailers and motor-homes, and then saw the sign advertising the Recreational Vehicle Sale and Convention. What can I say - She was gainfully employed and appeared to enjoy her choice of employment! Was this a field trip? Who am I to judge? She was a Happy Camper/Hooker? As the song goes, "Trailers for Sale or Rent ...!"

That evening I regaled Marnie with this story as we enjoyed our Martinis and had a scrumptious dinner at the Steakhouse. We were back to our room by midnight as we had a busy day planned for the next day. We are going to Memphis, TN (20 miles from Tunica) to visit Graceland and Elvis.

**A remedy to be shared:** When we were in Tunica, MS in August, 2010, the temperature was in the high 90s and very humid. As well, when we were outside, especially in the evening, the mosquitoes were very bad. We noticed that many of the outside workers and the bus drivers carried spray bottles which held a clear-looking liquid. When asked, what was in the bottles, we were told that it was a Listerine plus water mix, which was a cheap and effective bug-repellant. My mother always said, "You should learn something new every day or you have wasted a day!" I, too, now use the Mississippi Bug Mix and it works.

We were picked up from our Lobby at 9:00 a.m. by Blue Line Tours and took off for Graceland.

On our bus tour, we drove by the Lorraine Motel, the site where Martin Luther King was assassinated, on April 4,

1968. He was on the 2nd floor balcony when he was killed by a sniper's bullet.

## REV. MARTIN LUTHER KING JR.

Rev. Martin Luther King Jr. was a Baptist preacher and a famous civil rights leader in the U.S. He was a recipient of the Nobel Peace Prize, and will always be remembered for his "I Have a Dream Speech" which he gave at the Lincoln Memorial in Washington on August 28, 1963.

In March, 1969, he was on his way to Washington, but detoured to Memphis, TN to support a sanitation workers' strike.

On March 10, 1969, his accused assassin, James Earl Ray, a white man, pleaded guilty to his murder and was sentenced to 99 years in jail; he died in jail on April 23, 1998.

On October 16, 2011, the Martin Luther King Memorial dedication was held in Washington, DC. The huge, white, 30 foot statue made from granite blocks sits on a 4-acre site, cost $120 million and took 14 years to complete. On his statue the words "I Was a Drum Major for Justice Peace and Righteousness" are written. Many of his other famous quotes are written on the statue and on the Memorial Wall, such as:

**OUT OF A MONTAIN OF DESPAIR**

**A STONE OF HOPE**

Martin Luther King Jr. will always be remembered for his mission to fight for justice and equality. This memorial is the first to a black man on the Washington National Mall.

Thousands of people travelled to Washington for the dedication and many speakers spoke at the dedication. One speaker said: "He was a global citizen". His daughter, Bernice King, said:

* "We should never adjust to 1 percent of the people controlling 40 percent of the wealth."

* What a noteworthy statement based on the global demonstrations currently taking place in the financial districts/areas of many cities today. Financial insecurity is increasing because of the gap between the rich and the poor. The middle-class are being squeezed to the limit and taxes are really hurting the average worker and pensioners/retirees. The lack of jobs is a contributing factor to the unrest, and hopefully the politicians and governments are aware that the people are very concerned and expect more from their elected politicians.

**Million Dollar Question: Just how do you create the many jobs that are needed to employ so many that are unemployed? More government bureaucracy is not the answer.**

## ELVIS

The tour of Graceland/Mansion was certainly worth taking; the decor and design of each room was unique and very interesting.

Elvis was a very giving person and did not want to be known for his donations to the many charities and people he helped. There were checks chronically numbered and displayed in a showcase separate from the hundreds of awards and accolades that were very tastefully displayed in showcases in one area of the many hallway museums.

The award that Elvis was most proud of was the one he received from the United States Junior Chamber of Commerce (the Jaycees). He was chosen one of the Ten Outstanding Young Men of the Nation for 1970.

Elvis liked a famous *speech by Theodore Roosevelt and had a framed copy of it hanging in his private office upstairs at Graceland.

**The Man Who Counts**

**It is not the critic who counts, not the man who points out how the strong man tumbled, or where the doer of deeds could have done them better. The credit belongs to the man who is actually in the arena; whose face is marred by dust, sweat and blood; who strives valiantly; who errs and comes short again and again; who knows the great enthusiasms, the great devotions and spends himself in a worthy cause; who at the best knows in the end the triumph of high achievement, and who at the worst, if he fails, at least fails while daring greatly, so that his place shall never be with those cold and timid souls who know neither victory nor defeat.**

*I wrote down his speech for inclusion in this book.

His many famous costumes/outfits were elegantly displayed as well as his and Priscilla's wedding attire.

Elvis and Priscilla were married in 1967 and amicably divorced in 1973.

We toured his car museum (he purchased 14 Cadillac cars either for himself or friends). We saw his motorcycle collection and his own customized Jet plane (Hound Dog II), as well as the plane he bought for his daughter Lisa Marie, who was born in 1968 (The Lisa Marie).

The Mediation Garden

Elvis commissioned the design and construction of the Mediation Garden in 1965. In this beautiful garden there are four graves. The four graves are those of: Elvis Aaron Presley (January 8, 1935 – August 16, 1977), his mother – Gladys Love Smith Presley (April 25, 1912 – August 14, 1958), his father – Vernon Elvis Presley (April 10, 1916 – June 26, 1979), and his grandmother – Minnie May (Hood) Presley (June 17, 1890 – May 8, 1980). There is also a small marker of Elvis' twin brother Jessie Garon, who died at birth.

While at the grave site, many of the visitors placed candles and shed tears. This was very moving and demonstrated the affect the Mediation Garden and Elvis' memory had on the visitors.

I can now understand why Elvis had such a following of fans and as a legend he will always be remembered. He was only 42 years old when he died but he accomplished so much for such a young man.

A favorite saying, in one form or another, among fans today:

**"If you're an Elvis fan, then no words can explain.**

**If you are not an Elvis fan, then no words can suffice."**

This truly was a day well spent and of course, we brought back an Elvis souvenir.

That evening we had a casual dinner at the Toby Keith Bar on the 2$^{nd}$ floor of Harrah's. That too was enjoyable; we felt we were in Texas as this was a true western bar, and of course, music by Toby Keith was playing.

We left Tunica the next morning on a 10 a.m. flight back to Buffalo.

Another great adventure and fun was had by all. We shopped, gambled, enjoyed our wonderful meals and Martini's and came home with money! AND, visited Elvis's mansion. It doesn't get any better than that for two old/ladies (one 73 and the other 74)? Enjoy – Enjoy!

This was an excellent time of year to visit Graceland as it was not too crowded and allowed us to take our time touring, to read the many citations and to see so much of the Mansion and the surrounding grounds (two lovely horses silently meandering around the adjacent fields was also a bonus).

**NOTE:** On May 11, 2011, 9 casinos were closed in Tunica, MS because of the flooding of the Mississippi River. Many residents were evacuated and it would be a long time before life got back to normal in the State of Mississippi.

**THE TRULY RICH ARE THOSE WHO ENJOY WHAT THEY HAVE**

## TRIP TO PORTUGAL
## MAR. /2000

In March, 2000, I was invited to spend a 10-day vacation with Carmen (my old friend and travelling companion when we were single). She was there for three months and had rented a lovely condo-like apartment called the Ondamar Hotel Apartments in Albufeira in the Algarve. (Carmen lost her husband Joe, a few years before. Carmen was my Maid of Honor and Joe was an usher at our wedding in 1964).

The Algarve is a very popular tourist area, especially for Canadians and Albufeira is one of the many little towns that straddle the coast. What impressed me most about Albufeira was the tile work in the hotels, restaurants and even the streets and walkways. The tile work is spectacular and all done by hand. We saw workers on their hands and knees in the town square completing intricate tile work in, on and around buildings. They were meticulous and diligently worked to create beautiful designs on their projects. We saw magnificent pottery creations and other works of art as well.

The people were warm, friendly and happy. In the quaint little restaurants where we dined, the food was delicious and the service was excellent. One custom which was thoroughly enjoyed was when we paid our bill; the waiter brought us each a small glass of an excellent Port wine, in appreciation for our visit to their establishment. This happened each time we dined out, and it was a very nice custom which we appreciated and a fine way to finish off the dining experience.

One day, I decided to take a little bus trip to Portimao to visit the Algarve Casino. The bus trip along the coast was so interesting and the scenery and the little towns I went through made for great sight-seeing.

Unfortunately, when I got to the Casino, it wasn't open and would not open until 4:30 p.m. However, a very nice gentleman (Security) who was on the premises, offered to show me around and let me go into the Casino to have a quick look around. At that time, it was quite a small casino; there were slot machines scattered around with a few table games in the middle. (I understand that now there is a beautiful hotel with an expanded Casino facility on the site).

Even though I didn't get to play in the casino in Portimao, after dinner that evening in our hotel, they had Bingo (I have never been a Bingo player) however, this was the evening entertainment, so off we went to play. This turned out to be a real fun evening; Carmen won three times, I won twice; (I forget what we won) but we had a great time meeting other hotel guests, from various parts of the world, and just enjoyed the whole experience. I do remember one of us won a bottle of wine and we shared it with our table.

I feel fortunate to have been able to visit Portugal, and this was another trip that turned out to be a truly enjoyable vacation, thanks to Carmen.

# THE ROAD OF LIFE CAN LEAD TO MANY PLACES – ENJOY!

## The Junkets

I have received a few complimentary 3-or 4-night stays. The 'comps' were for:

Las Vegas (airfare extra), at choice of one of Harrah's properties; these properties were Bally's, Caesars, Flamingo Las Vegas, Harrah's, Imperial Palace, Paris and or Rio All-Suite Hotel & Casino.

4-day stay, including airfare and hotel transfers (out of Buffalo Niagara International Airport) at a Harrah's hotel in Tunica, Mississippi, for $319 (for myself and a guest).

4-day stay, including airfare and hotel transfers (out of Buffalo International Airport) at Harrah's in Laughlin, Nevada, for US$440 (for myself and a guest).

Most casinos send "Happy Birthday" cards to their members with a bonus gift for slot play (from $5.00 and up) or you could receive an invitation to the special quarterly Birthday Party put on by the casino. Seneca Niagara is one casino that puts on these party bashes and they are great. I had the opportunity to attend two of these over the years; one on my 70th Birthday, and the last one in May, 2011, my 73rd Birthday.

A BIRTHDAY JOKE

Scotch with two drops of Water

A lady goes to the bar on a cruise ship and orders a Scotch with two drops of water.

As the bartender gives her the drink, she says, "I'm on this cruise to celebrate by 80th birthday and it's today…"

The bartender says, "Well, since it's your birthday, I'll buy you a drink. In fact, this one is on me."

As the woman finishes her drink, the woman to her right says, "I would like to buy you a drink, too."

The old woman says, "Thank you. Bartender, I will have a Scotch with two drops of water."

"Coming up", says the Bartender.

As she finishes that drink, the man to her left says, "I would like to buy you one, too."

The old woman says, "Thank you. Bartender, I want another Scotch with two drops of water."

"Coming right up," the Bartender says.

As he gives her the drink, he says, "Ma'am, I'm dying of curiosity. Why the Scotch with only two drops of water?"

The old woman replies, "Sonny, when you're my age, you've learned to hold your liquor. Holding your water, however, is a whole other issue."

**THE BIRTHDAY BASH – May, 2011**

**Gail and I**

Let the fun begin!

There was a one-half hour pre-dinner cocktail party where wine and beer was served, delicious appetizers, a lovely dinner, and great entertainment. Hats/Crowns and noise-makers were on all the white linen-covered tables. This party had a Mexican theme and the table centre-pieces were hand created of fresh flowers arranged in Martini cactus-stemmed glasses. How original. The waiters and waitresses served the food wearing white gloves, and the service was excellent. After dinner, the lights were dimmed and all servers came out at the same time carrying a Birthday cake with sparklers for each table. They cut the cake and served each diner individually. Draw prizes of $300 each were won. Very impressive and well done! It was a great evening and we thoroughly enjoyed the Birthday Bash.

Gail lost her husband, Jack, in 2009.

# COUNT YOUR AGE BY FRIENDS – NOT YEARS. COUNT YOUR LIFE BY SMILES – NOT TEARS

## UNEXPECTED GET-AWAY 'COMP'

When we were single, we used to ski in Ellicottville, NY, and continued for a few years after we were married. I had always thought it would be great to go back in the summer or fall to see how things had changed. In late September, 2009, my husband and I decided to take a little trip back to Ellicottville.

Seneca Allegany Casino in Salamanca, NY (casino owned by the Seneca Gaming Commission) is only about 12 miles from Ellicottville.

I called Seneca Allegany and asked for a Host/Hostess. I asked if I could get a 'comp' room for two nights in October. She requested my Player's Card number, and I gave her my Seneca Niagara Card number. She looked me up and said, "You are requesting a 'comp' room but you have never been here!" "That is correct," said I, "but we would like to visit the Allegany Casino to see how we like it." She then checked the dates I requested, and said, "Yes, those two nights are available," and that is how I received this 'comp'.

We had a lovely three-day trip to Ellicottville. On the way, we stopped and explored the little ski-town and saw how the area had built up, had lunch, did some shopping and enjoyed Ellicottville in the fall season.

When we stayed at Allegany, we had a lovely room, great meals and met some very nice people.

My husband,* "who doesn't gamble", put $5.00 in a five cent machine the day we arrived. He hit two Bonus games and won $200.00. He came to the table where I was playing Blackjack, showed me his ticket, cashed it in, and went back to the room to relax. He did not play anymore, kept his winnings, and of course, was a happy camper! I played the tables, a few slot machines and ended up winning $80.00.

The Casino is located in an area with a beautiful background of mountains and trees. At that time of year, the leaves were in full color, and the weather was still warm; we thoroughly enjoyed the last outburst of summer. A day later, when we were leaving, there was a heavy fog and a snowstorm warning was in effect for late afternoon and evening.

*See: "Statements I Have Heard" at the end of the book.

Later that winter, I received promotion material called SLOPES & SLOTS –"Bring in your ski lift ticket once every promotional week to receive $15.00 free slot play." Very creative advertising.

### LAS VEGAS 'COMP'

In August, 2011, I received a 'comp' offer from Harrah's. Their offer included up to four free nights (for 2) at a choice of these hotels: Harrah's, Rio All Suite Hotel, Bally's, Imperial Palace, and the Flamingo.

This offer was good from September 9, 2011 to December 29, 2011.

In September, 2011, West Jet Airlines had a seat sale, flying out of Hamilton, ON.

Gail and I, decided to book the 4-night junket at the Flamingo Hotel and flew out of Hamilton, which was very convenient for both of us. The flight to Las Vegas cost $458 each and included all taxes.

We invited Gail's friend Annetta, who lived in California, to come for a visit and she stayed with us for three days. Can you imagine three 70-plus year-olds on the loose in Las Vegas?

The weather was beautiful; 94 degrees but without humidity. We toured the strip and visited the newer casinos. I did not play any tables at the newer Casinos as the ante was too high ($25 and up). However, we played a few slot machines, enjoyed the touring, and had a great lunch at Toby Keith's Bar and Grill located in Harrah's casino. We did a little shopping and had free drinks at the Casinos where we visited. Actually, Gail won at the slots, Annetta lost and I lost, but we just had a blast of a time.

One thing about Las Vegas, there is always something to do, somewhere to go and the food is very good. I spent two mornings at the beautiful large Flamingo pool where the people-watching was something else. I cannot believe the large women who think going topless or wearing the briefest of bikinis is okay. Wow! – Ladies look in a mirror; what you see is not good! I also saw many "breast enhancements"; not that I was looking, but a few of them just could not be missed. They actually looked like white 5-pin bowling balls!

### The Pai Gow Experience

The third night at the Flamingo, I decided to try playing the Pai Gow Poker game. I had never played this game before and was told that it was an interesting game. I sat in at a $5 table, bought $100 in chips, and played for two hours.

In this game, the player is dealt seven cards, must pick a high hand, and a low hand and plays against the dealer. The idea is to pick the best hand or high card and place it in the 'High Hand' slot and then pick the two best cards left and place them in the Low Hand slot. If you are not sure what to pick, the dealer will and can help you. There is another spot called 'Envy', which when played costs an additional $5.00 but gives the player a chance to win a bonus pay-out should you or another player happen to get dealt a 'money-hand' such as a Straight or better. I put $5.00 in the Envy spot.

It was around 12:30 a.m. and I was down $60 and decided it was time to turn in. I ordered a Scotch on the rocks (to help me sleep as I had not had great sleeps since arriving in Las Vegas; when you are old, sleep patterns are not the best). Of course, Las Vegas never sleeps either.

While waiting for my drink, I play one more hand, and that is when a gentleman at the table gets a seven card straight flush! What excitement. The man is from Victoria, B.C. and his wife, two daughters and sons 'in-law have been standing behind him watching him play. The dealer announces that he has won $5000, and the rest of the players who played the 'Envy' slot will receive a $500 bonus. By now we are all clapping, laughing and jumping around. It takes awhile for us to get paid, as they had to check the cards, the cameras upstairs, and then someone in a suit came to pay him. As well, because he is Canadian, 30% of the payout is withheld, and he receives $3500 in chips, and the paperwork to show proof of the withheld taxes.

There is a lovely little lady sitting beside me and she and I are both very happy to receive our $500 bonus. It is at this point that we realized that the other man at the table had not played the 'Envy' spot and therefore he is not eligible for the $500 bonus. He leaves the table and I am sure he is still talking to himself for not paying the extra $5.00.

I then happily go to my room. I didn't win the hand but someone else did and I got paid. That is a win! Happiness is!

The last full day in Las Vegas, I spent the morning at the pool, and Gail and Annetta hit the strip to do some shopping. They did their thing and we all met in the room at 6:00 p.m. to get ready for dinner.

I enjoyed the pool, had lunch at the pool Patio and then showered, dressed and went out to the "The Strip." I picked up a few souvenirs from the interesting street vendors and then paid a visit to O'Sheas. This is a small casino adjacent to the Flamingo where my husband and I, daughter, son-in-law and his parents all visited when we were there several years ago. It is a fun casino where there are $5.00 tables for Blackjack, 3-Card Plus Poker and Let It Ride. They also had $25.00 buy-in Texas Hold Em Poker.

I sat at a $5.00 Blackjack table and played for about an hour. Every time the ladies at the table won, the dealer would give us a string of 'lucky beads'. We had a great time, and I ended up wearing seven strings of lucky beads when I left the table.

While at the table, I had the opportunity to talk to the dealer Shawn. He was a very nice young man from Ohio. He had just moved to Las Vegas in January, 2011. He said he had lost his job in Ohio (worked in a manufacturing plant) and that jobs were very difficult to find back home. He did not like the Ohio winters and decided to move to Las Vegas. He was hired by Harrah's and is now a dealer at O'Shea's. He loves his job and the climate. When he hears the resident people complaining about the heat, he laughs, and says the climate is perfect for him. Not that much humidity, a dry heat, and winters that can't be as cold as back in Ohio.

I spoke with a Floor Manager, and he told me that O'Sheas probably would not be there by next year. They would be tearing it down to rebuild something else associated with the Flamingo or Harrah's. I am happy that I had a last visit as it was one of the smaller casinos where people really enjoyed themselves.

The last night we were there, we enjoyed the Flamingo Buffet; I had received two free Buffets with the 'comp', so

Gail and I used the coupon and Annetta used her accumulated points for her Buffet. We thoroughly enjoyed the Buffet with many choices of food, e.g., shrimp, lobster, roast beef, turkey, ham, and a huge selection of vegetables. Delicious desserts too.

After dinner, we decided to sit down at another Pai Gow Poker table and we played there for two hours. At one point, Gail got a Straight Flush and won $250 and Annetta and I both received a $25 bonus. That is when we all should have left. We were all ahead but stayed too long. The dealer was getting very good hands and was beating us. I had been ahead about $65 but stayed and started to lose. I finally left the table with the money I started with plus $12.00. Not a loss but not a great win either.

All in all, the Las Vegas trip was enjoyable and we did have fun. All three of us left as losers. Between the winning and losing, over the four days/nights, I lost about $400 and Gail the same. I am not sure how much Annetta lost but she was down too she said. To add to her losing woes, she had won $149.00 the night before, thought she had put it in her purse, but when she arrived at the room, the money was not there. That hurts!

**Lesson Learned: You can win a little and lose a lot if you stay too long!**

While visiting Caesars, I picked up their Responsible Gaming brochure which outlined their Code of Commitment.

More than two decades ago, they became the first casino company to create a responsible gaming program. They educate their employees about responsible gaming, and encourage their customers to play responsibly.

Their brochure outlines signs of When Gambling Might Be a Problem:

(20 Questions from their brochure)

While the following is not a diagnostic test and should not be used as such, many people who have called gambling help lines have answered yes to one or more of the following questions:

1. Do you lose time from work due to gambling?
2. Is gambling making your home life unhappy?
3. Is gambling affecting your reputation?
4. Have you ever felt remorse after gambling?
5. Do you ever gamble to get money to help pay debts or to otherwise solve financial difficulties?
6. Does gambling cause a decrease in your ambition or efficiency?
7. After losing, do you feel you must return as soon as possible and win back your losses?
8. After a win, do you have a strong urge to return and win more?
9. Do you often gamble until your last dollar is gone?
10. Do you ever borrow to finance your gambling?
11. Have you ever sold any real or personal property to finance gambling?
12. Are you reluctant to use "gambling money" for normal expenditures?
13. Does gambling make you careless of the welfare of your family?
14. Do you ever gamble longer than you had planned?
15. Do you ever gamble to escape worry or trouble?
16. Have you ever committed or considered committing an illegal act to finance gambling?
17. Does gambling cause you to have difficulty sleeping?

18. Do arguments, disappointments, or frustrations create an urge to gamble?

19. Do you have an urge to celebrate any good fortune by a few hours of gambling?

20. Have you ever considered self-destruction as a result of your gambling?

*Caesars do have programs in place that allow a customer to restrict certain casino privileges, such as credit, check cashing, mail outs, or casino play.

For additional information: www.caesars.com/about us/ code of commitment /index.html

*All casinos in Canada and the U.S. have similar programs in place.

**A SIGN OF STRENGTH IS TO ADMIT A WEAKNESS**

♣ ♦ ♥ ♠

# CHAPTER 9
# SLOTS, POTS and JACKPOTS

# SLOTS/POTS AND JACKPOTS

## FEB. /2003

## THE WINS AND LOSSES

### THE BIG TABLE WINS

**MY FIRST BIG WIN – Brantford Casino, Brantford, ON**

In 2003, the Brantford Casino had off-track betting. My husband, Len, is not a casino person and he likes to put a few dollars on the horses, (he likes the horses and his usual bet is $2.00 to $4.00 a race; if on a very rare occasion he does venture into the casino, his maximum spent is $10).

He went to the off-track lounge while I went to the casino area and sat at a $5.00 Caribbean Stud table game. I sat down and played four hands of Caribbean Stud poker when I got the Straight Flush. A Straight Flush pays 10% of the Progressive Jackpot. I looked up at the Progressive Jackpot monitor and it read approximately $67,990. In order to receive 10% of the Progressive Jackpot, one must play the extra $1.00, and if a player happens to be dealt a Royal Flush, he/she will receive 100% of the Jackpot, if the $1.00 has been played.

What excitement. It took awhile for me to get paid as many things have to be checked. Apparently the cameras above check that all was above-board when the hand was dealt, and all cards must be checked and accounted for before you get paid. If the dealer opens with an Ace and King, or better, then the players with winning hands who stayed in the game (must beat the dealer's hand) get paid on the Ante and the double down bet. For my win, the dealer did not open but because I had played the extra dollar on the Progressive Jackpot, I get paid.

While waiting to be paid, a gentleman at the table asked if I would like him to locate my husband. I said "Oh yes, please look for him in the off-track lounge." He found my husband and brought him back to the table but didn't tell him why. My husband saw all the people standing around and thought I had had a heart attack. I was paid in chips and then went to the Cashier and asked for and received a check for $6800! Needless to say, it was a lucrative casino moment and I shared the wealth and gave my husband $2000. A part share of the wealth so to speak.

My husband cashed a race ticket for $6.40 and we then left the casino and went and had a wonderful dinner to celebrate.

Note: The Brantford Casino has just completed a $39 million dollar renovation which included an addition (the expanded Poker Room) and it took approximately 3 years to complete. Many trades were used in this renovation which meant employment for skilled and unskilled labor. Renovations are continually going on in the Casino industry which creates employment.

**A BIG SLOT WIN**

**FEB. /2009**

My husband Len, and I went over to Niagara Falls to shop and as I had a comp room and tickets for the entertainment, we stayed overnight at the Casino.

After breakfast the next morning, I had chips to cash in from the night before. I told my husband that I also would like 10 minutes to play a penny slot machine. He said he would meet me in the Lobby in half an hour.

I cashed in my chips and on my way back to the Lobby I sat down at a slot machine called 'Vibrant 7s'. I had spent $7.00 when I got the bonus of free games. During the bonus, I got an additional chance on a numbered game bonus which could result in winning a jackpot. I did hit the Jackpot and of course was very excited. However, I had to wait for a Floor Attendant to come to pay me. I knew my husband was waiting and was thinking he will wonder where I am; I had better go and tell him. The lady beside me said, 'Oh don't leave your machine until the floor person gets to you.

When the lady Attendant arrived, I asked if she would wait at the machine until I went and got my husband. There was no problem and, of course, when I went to get him, he said, "You're late", I know said I, "but I won and am waiting to get paid." He then did not mind waiting for me to get paid.

As the slot win was $1,419.00, there were withholding taxes of 30% or $425.70. I was escorted to the Cashier's location, where the taxes were taken, given a receipt for the amount of taxes withheld and received the remainder in cash. I was happy to receive US$993.30. A great win for a 10-minute stint at the Vibrant 7s' machine.

## A BIGGER TABLE WIN

### Nov. /2009

My friend Gail and I went shopping in Niagara Falls, NY and took advantage of a Seneca Niagara Falls overnight room-comp. We arrived at the Casino at about 4 p.m., had a drink in the room and then went downstairs for an hour of play before going to dinner. She played the slots and I played the tables.

## TABLE WIN – CARIBBEAN STUD

I joined a Caribbean Stud table where the ante was $5.00. After playing about half an hour, I was even (I have the money I started with). There were five other gentlemen at the table when I got into the game. One by one they were leaving as they were losing. There were three of us left and I was also thinking about leaving to go to the Blackjack table. The dealer dealt the hand and when I picked up mine, I saw the 4, 3, 5 and the Ace of Clubs, and then I saw the 2 of Clubs. Wow, I had a straight flush. I looked at the above monitor and saw that the Progressive Jackpot was around $127,700. I couldn't believe it. The dealer then opened with a pair of Aces. Great, I now will get 10% of the Progressive Jackpot. As well, because the dealer opened, I will get paid on the backup bet which is 50 to 1 odds/$500.

The dealer said he could not believe that I was so calm. I replied, "I haven't been paid yet!" We laughed. I was then paid $500 (50 to 1 odds on the backup bet plus the $5.00 ante) and then later, got paid 10% of the Progressive Jackpot.

The process of being paid the Progressive Jackpot:

Two floor bosses checked all the cards and the overhead cameras also checked the last two hands played. Once I was declared a winner, I was escorted to a small room in the Casino where two Accountants prepared the paperwork. There is a 30% withholding tax on Jackpot table wins. Before taxes, the total Progressive win was $12,742.37. Federal taxes withheld were $3,822.71. When asked if I wanted cash, I said no a Cashier check would be fine. The Accountant said, "I'll give you a Casino check, our checks are good." I was also given a Form 1042-S for the IRS. This is a "Foreign Person's Source Income Subject to Withholding form" which shows the win and the taxes withheld. I received my check for $8919.66 and needless to say, this was an awesome win.

As a foreign citizen (Canadian) in order to receive taxes withheld, one must apply to the IRS at the end of the fiscal year. The can be done by oneself or you can use one of many companies who charge a fee to recover the withheld taxes. For additional information, see Chapter 10, Casino Tax Rebates vs. Government Tax Laws.

That evening Gail and I enjoyed another wonderful dinner at *The Western Door Steakhouse and the Martinis and of course, dinner was on me.

After dinner, I put $20 in a penny machine called "The White Orchid", and hit a bonus game and won another $750. My total winnings for that casino visit were $10,000 – a very exciting win!

I must mention the Staff at the Western Door Steakhouse. The Hosts/Hostesses: Bruce, Richard and Janine (these are the ones I know by name) are the most pleasant and accommodating people. The servers/waiters/waitresses are the best in the business (Hal, John, Kathy, Kristen, Melanie, Michelle, Sharon, Steve, Stephen, Dave and the others who know us). The food is excellent, and The Western Door

Steakhouse is rated as one of the best in western New York State and has won many awards.

Note: We used to own The Commercial Hotel in for Port Dover, ON (in a partnership for 12 years) and we always emphasized pleasant customer service. I truly believe the success of any business is based on customer service. Dealing with the public isn't always easy, but attitude and commitment to your job makes the job easier and more rewarding. Product knowledge is very important as well. Enjoy the job and when you are pleasant, the clients/customers usually reciprocate.

## A BIGGER SLOT WIN

### MAY/2011

The morning after the Birthday Bash, to which we were invited, I went downstairs to play the tables for an hour before I met Gail for breakfast. While walking into the casino, I noticed new slot machines that I had not seen before.

**CHINA SHORES** – this was a one-cent machine and I ordered a coffee and sat down to play. I put in $20, played forty cents, then sixty cents and then accidentally hit the 225 button which meant I was betting $2.25 in a penny machine! Before I realized what happened, I won bonus games, and then more bonus games, and even more bonus games. In total, I won 151 bonus games! I thought I would be there forever as I couldn't believe that many games could be won.

## LET THE GAMES BEGIN

Well the excitement of it all. By now, I had a small group of people behind me watching the action. With the winning games accumulating, the winnings were up over $1,000. People were commenting, "Oh my, if the total goes over $1200, you will have 30% of the win withheld in taxes." By now, I am *praying not to win any more and still had 8 games left to play. I am also thinking, what if the machine has malfunctioned and I won't get paid. The stress of it all! All went well, and by the last game, the total win was $1,198.50. I immediately cashed out and met Gail and off we went for breakfast. Excitement at its peak with the China Panda Bears!

\* I have been told that more praying goes on in a casino than in any Church.

**THE LOSSES**

**EASY COME—EASY GO**

**OCT. /2009**

It is early morning (8:30 am). I like playing early in the morning as the casino is quieter and the players are usually 'more stabilized'. I joined a $10 blackjack table and sat down at the first spot to the right of the dealer. After looking around the table, a noticed a young man with a huge stack of chips and he is playing two hands at $100 per hand. He was asked by another player how much he had won and he announced that he had won $10,000 playing 'Texas Hold Em Poker' (he had been playing all night).

He was losing and then he doubled and sometimes tripled his bets (from $200 to $300 per hand). As I sat there playing for 35 minutes, he kept losing. I couldn't believe his bad luck or the logic for his betting. I kept thinking why doesn't he just leave, try another table or at least reduce his bet. We are at a $10 table! He finally left and he lost $6000 in 40 minutes, and upon leaving he said, "Well, at least I am up $4000. Was this a positive side? A definite downside!

**KNOW WHEN TO GO**

I too, have lost at the casino. The biggest loss on a single visit has been $300. I lost $200 at the tables, and $100 in the slots. The biggest loss on a 4-day junket was $400. This was of course, very unsettling. As stated, before, you must know your limit. When you have reached your 'loss limit' then it is time to walk away. You can always come back another time. The casino/s will still be there. Keep a journal, list your wins and losses; in other words, keep your own Win/

Loss Statement. This form of entertainment can become very expensive, and like any form of entertainment, should be factored into your entertainment budget.

Remember: You don't visit a Casino to get rich!

## AN UNEXPECTED LOSS

While on one of our junkets, I mistakenly gave a waitress a US$100 tip. We had dinner and each had our *usual Martini with dinner. After dinner I sat down at a penny slot machine. A waitress came by and asked for drink orders. I asked for a coffee with Bailey's Irish Cream (I normally do not drink when I am gambling nor do I smoke; I am a social drinker). As mentioned before, customers/players do not pay for drinks in the U.S. casinos. Anyway, I gave her what I thought was a $1.00 tip, and did not discover until later that I had given her a $100! (From then on, I always keep my $1.00 bills in a separate compartment for tipping if needed). This was a very expensive lesson learned and I am sure the waitress was skipping through her shift for the rest of the evening. As well, after that big 'tipping' lesson, I only order water or a hot tea after dinner, when I am at a table.

*We are known as the "007 Martini ladies" at the Western Door Steakhouse, Seneca Niagara Casino.

## PRACTICE MAKES PERFECT, SO BE CAREFUL WHAT YOU PRACTICE

## HOW LUCKY CAN YOU GET

A few years ago, my husband Len and I took a *day-trip on the Casino Bus to the Niagara Fallsview Casino. It is a beautiful Casino that is situated right by the Falls. We have been there on a couple of day trips; the Falls are awesome at any time of year but the most spectacular view of the Falls is in the spring. When seated in the Dining area by the windows, you can see the most breathtaking ice formations at the bottom of the Falls - an artist's dream.

On this particular trip, we had taken the early morning bus and arrived at the Casino by 9 a.m. The plan was for me to meet him at 11:30 a.m., by the Buffet entrance. While I went to look around the Casino, Len went to have a coffee and read his paper (as stated before, he doesn't gamble).

I eventually sat down at a 3-card Poker table, played a bit, and moved to a Blackjack table and by 11 a.m. I was up $200. It is time to leave to meet Len. I cashed in my chips and asked for two Black chips ($100 each), and put them in my jacket pocket. I leave for the Cashier window and when I get there, I only have one Black chip in my pocket! Oh woe is me; I have lost a $100 chip! I am now in panic mode and the only thing to do is retrace my steps. How does one retrace their steps in a Casino? Finding the Washroom is a challenge for me; I even ended up in a broom closet once because I couldn't find the Exit from the Washroom. I know, I know, not everyone is area-observant. Anyway, I am trying to retrace my steps back to the table that I had left. The Casino carpet had many colors in it, and looking for a Black chip, never mind finding it, is in my mind not going to happen - someone would have spotted it and of course would keep it. Who would turn in a $100 chip to Lost and Found? I am just about half-way to the table, when I look down, and there on a black area of the carpet is my $100 chip! Now if that isn't luck, I don't know what is. I get to the Buffet entrance just in time in meet Len. Did I tell him about the win-loss-win Chip hunt? No. He can read about it!

## WHEN IS TOO MUCH INFORMATION JUST TOO MUCH INFORMATION?

Casinos have created many jobs in the Transportation Industry, i.e., bus drivers, tour operators, and related jobs (hosts/hostesses meeting buses on their arrivals/departures, scheduling personnel for the daily trips and the 3-4 day bus trips to other Casinos. Vehicle maintenance is another area for employment which is worthy of consideration.

## CASINO TIPPING

When at a casino, I always tip the waiter or waitress when I order a tea, coffee or a soft drink. I do not order any alcoholic drink if I am at a Canadian casino (the drinks are just too expensive). If at a U.S. Casino (drinks are free), and I happen to order a drink at a game table, I always tip $1.00. I like to order a Scotch and water on occasion or maybe a draft beer. The tips are appreciated, and of the few floor servers I have asked, they have said they usually make on average $50 - $100 per shift on tips.

Canadian casinos now have Self-Serve areas where you can get your own liquid refreshments (excluding alcohol).

**Tipping on Wins**

Players tip dealers for good hands and are expected to tip when they win a big hand or a jackpot. I have seen big winners tip up to $100 and have heard of $500 or more being given when Progressive jackpots are won. When I asked one person if they tipped, he answered "No, I don't tip, why should I tip; the dealers don't give me money when I'm losing, why I should I tip when I win?" The most I have tipped at the tables is $100.

Interestingly, I have received $100 twice from table winners. Both times, these gentlemen won over $10,000 and they tipped the dealer and then gave each player at the table a $100. That too was very surprising but certainly appreciated. I still have those $100 tips stashed away.

Some people also tip the Floor Attendant for Slot machine wins. Again, the tip depends on the amount won and the generosity of the player. The most I have tipped on a slot win is $10.

**A ROYAL WIN**

**JUNE/1961**

When I was 23 years old, and single, I was invited to go on a Blind Date to the Queen's Plate at Woodbine Racetrack in Toronto. This is Canada's most prestigious race and is held every June. My date was Romeo and we went with two other couples and had tickets for the Club House. What a great day it was with the ladies wearing their fine frocks and beautiful hats, and the men in splendid 'club attire'. I remember wearing a mauve sundress and clipped several *red feathers to a small hat frame (today that type of hat is known as a 'Fascinator'; remember Kate and William's Royal Wedding).

After wining and dining, just before the big race, Romeo asked me what horse I was betting on. I said, "I am betting on the Canadian thoroughbred 'Blue Light'. He said, "You're kidding, it is going off at 50 to 1 odds." "That is the horse I am betting", said I. Well, what a race it was and yes, Blue Light won and paid me a handsome sum for my $2.00 bet. I was the only one at the table who bet that lovely horse. I liked the name too. How does one pick a horse? I heard a man say, "Just put a pin in the program and if you pick a winner, you're lucky."

I mention this story because it does relate to gambling and for years after my husband and I were married, we would attend the Queen's Plate with friends Barbara and Tony.

Who knew then that 50 years later, I would be one of those *Red Hat ladies. We wear purple outfits and red hats to all our outings. I belong to the Hamilton H'Attitudes and they are just a fantastic bunch of ladies. We have a great time and besides enjoying our monthly outings, we also donate to Food Drives and support other charities, and yes, the odd trip to the Casino for the dining, entertainment and a bit of gambling for those who wish to partake.

* "When I am an old woman, I shall wear purple." by Jenny Joseph

### THE FALL FAIR

### (a Fall sometime in the 1980s)

Years ago, my husband, Len, daughter Kelly and I, loved to attend the Fall Fairs in Ancaster, Binbrook, Caledonia, and other surrounding areas.

The one I particularly remember was the Ancaster Fair at the old fairgrounds in Ancaster. Len and I liked to bet on the trotters at these fairs and I will never forget my big win at the Fair.

## THE RACE IS ON/WHO NEEDS A PROGRAM?

At race time, Len met me in the stands and he had purchased only one program; I was somewhat miffed as I thought we both should have a program. Anyway, I bet the daily double (first and second race). My double won and paid $21.80. I happily leave the stands to collect my money and when I returned, Len wasn't there. I quickly went back down to the betting lineup to make my bet on the third race. I think it was the third or it could have been the fourth race (it was a long time ago), and I did not see Len in the lineup nor did I have a program. I was standing behind a man who was holding his program high enough for me to have a quick glance at the entries, and I just picked the numbers 7 and 8 for a $2.00 Exactor, not reading or seeing any pertinent information (as if it helps).

I went back up to the stands to watch the race; Len still hadn't returned. The race is over and the horses came in 8 and 7. Darn – I lost. Then an announcement is made that there is an inquiry and to hold all tickets. The inquiry took some time and then they announced that the official winner was 7 and the number 8 horse was second. Wow – I have an exactor! They did not announce the payouts.

I leave the stands and go back down to stand in the lineup with my ticket. At that time, they had a small screen-monitor set up near the front of the line where you could see the payouts. I quickly glanced at the Exactor payout and thought I saw $98 and some cents. Great, what a nice win. Just as I was getting up to the wicket, they made the announcement that the Exactor paid $981.50. Well, now I am very excited, to say the least. When I got to the wicket, a gentleman behind the wicket asked me to go to the side entrance and he escorted me into the area where the cashiers were working. He had to collect money from all the cashiers, and the money had to be counted out and checked two or three times, and then he paid me. I stuffed the money in my purse as there were several $20s, $50s, etc. to make up the amount. I skip back to the stands where Len is now sitting.

Before I had a chance to say anything, Len says, "Did you see that race? I thought I had the exactor and then they had the inquiry and there went my ticket." I said, "Guess what, I had the 7 and 8 ticket" and I then opened my purse and said, "Look at the payout!" Just then they announced the $981.50 payout for the 7/8 Exactor again and said: "Ladies and Gentlemen — there was only one ticket holder." Len couldn't believe it. What a Fall Fair — I won over $1000 that afternoon; it certainly wasn't knowledge about horses or riders – it was strictly good luck and no program.

Incidentally, that win ticket paid two installments on our house taxes for that year.

**TAMPA, FLORIDA**

**Spring Break, 1977**

**A DOG'S DAY NIGHT**

**DERBY LANES and the GREYHOUNDS**

In 1997, while vacationing in Treasure Island, Florida, Len and I decided to go to the evening races at the Dog Track at Derby Lanes, Tampa, FL. Neither of us had been before and really didn't know what to expect.

At first, I was quite concerned about Greyhounds chasing a rabbit on a stick until Len said, "It's not a real rabbit they are chasing; it's a white flag on a stick." "Oh fine, now let's get a program, bet a dog and let the races begin." We were betting $2.00 a race and not winning. How do you pick a dog? The races go so quickly and the poor dogs are yelping and howling and look very under-nourished to me.

It is the last race and I hadn't cashed a ticket. Len had a couple of Place and Show tickets that he cashed. I decided to bet a Trifecta, which means the picking of three dogs which must come in First, Second and Third. Len says,

"You can't even pick one dog, and you are betting on three!" "Yes," I said, "I am betting a $2.00 Trifecta on the numbers 2, 4 and 6 and hoping for the best. I didn't even look at the program. Dogs are like people; they either feel like running or they don't. Who do you ask and how can you tell? Well, the race is on and before I can blink an eye, the race is over. I look at the results posted on the track screen, and what do you know, they came in 2, 4 and 6. When the results were posted, the Trefecta paid US$289.00. Now I am howling and yelping in delight. The Canadian dollar was lower than the U.S. at the time, so, of course, we are happy with the U.S. win. We were leaving the next day, and had enjoyed a wonderful vacation, fun in the sun, and a lucrative night out with the Dogs.

♣ ♦ ♥ ♠

# CHAPTER 10
# CASINO TAX REBATES vs. GOVT. TAX LAWS

### CASINO TAX REBATES vs. GOVERNMENT TAX LAWS

There are no taxes withheld if one wins a jackpot or a large amount of money in a Canadian casino.

### US WITHHOLDING TAX LAWS

The Internal Revenue Service requires that casinos and other gambling establishments withhold 30% of the gambling winnings of international visitors. However, due to the US Canada Tax Treaty, Canadians can offset gambling losses against the gambling winnings reported on Form 1042-S and get some or all of the withheld taxes back. Non US citizens that are residents of certain other countries may also qualify for a refund of the 30% withholding on their Casino winnings.

In addition to Canada the following other listed countries qualify: Austria, Czech Republic, Denmark, Finland, France, Germany, Hungary, Ireland, Italy, Japan, Latvia, Lithuania, Luxembourg, Netherlands, Russian Federation, Slovak Republic, Slovenia, South Africa, Spain, Sweden, Tunisia, Turkey, Ukraine, and the United Kingdom. These listed countries do not have to establish gambling losses in order to claim a full refund.

A non-resident must apply for an IRS Individual Taxpayer Identification Number. This is done by obtaining and filling in Form W-7, which is issued by the Department of the

Treasury Internal Revenue Service. I could have contacted the IRS and obtained the W-7 Form myself, but chose to use an agent who handled all the paperwork from start to finish.

An IRS authorized Certifying Acceptance Agent (with a registered ID#) can get an Individual Taxpayer Identification Number and provide you with the services required for tax recovery.

I chose to use a Canadian company: Casino Tax Rebate in Thunder Bay, ON and was very pleased with their service. They were established in 1979, are members of the Better Business Bureau, and an IRS Certifying Acceptance Agent. They have an established reputation in Canada and I was very pleased with the handling of my claim. As of this writing, according to their website, the largest tax recovery for a client was $53,225.46. Their fee was reasonable as well.

Before applying for the Tax rebate, one must provide Win/Loss Statements from the casino/s where you gambled in the US. You can only request these statements at the end of the fiscal year in which you won the money. Win/Loss Statements can be obtained from any casino where one has gambled, as long as the Player's Card for that casino was used. All Win/Loss Statements submitted are used to calculate and determine the amount you are eligible to receive back. You may receive a full refund or a partial refund; the amount is based on the Total Winnings and Losses from the Win/Loss Statements provided.

From the time all the necessary paperwork was submitted, it took approximately 4 weeks to receive my tax rebate. I did not get the full amount back as I did not have enough losses.

Note: The IRS has specific requirements that relate to the claiming of gambling wins and losses. Additional information pertaining to these requirements is available in IRS Publication 529 or at the IRS website: http://www.irs.gov/topics/tc419.html

♣ ♦ ♥ ♠

# CHAPTER 11
## THE DOWN SIDE

From research and my own experiences, I believe that there are two types of gamblers. There is the one who goes to the casino for entertainment and sets aside an amount of money for this outing, and the other type who becomes an addicted gambler. Just as there are social drinkers vs. alcoholics, an occasional smoker vs. a "chimney", or obesity from over-eating, when the attraction becomes a harmful habit and turns into an addiction, therein lies a problem. The Down Side stories which follow are from those who recognized and admitted they had a problem.

**THE DOWN SIDE**

Unfortunately, as with any addiction, gambling can be a devastating one. I was able to interview a few people who were willing to share their stories of addiction. This is Rhonda's story.

**Rhonda**

Rhonda was 19 when she first visited an Ontario casino to celebrate her 19th birthday with her friends.

She played Roulette and placed a $25 bet on a number which paid 35 to 1 and she said she won $900. This was the beginning of becoming hooked. She also bought lotto tickets, scratch tickets and played Pro Line at the time.

She was in University at the time and was an excellent student. She was able to knock off essays and term papers without much studying and had a lot of spare time on her hands. She lived at home and worked part-time as a bartender. She was paid an allowance (from her father) and was allowed to keep all her earned money and did not pay room or board at home. She had a boyfriend who was not a student, had a well-paying job (worked shifts) and he also liked to gamble. It was not unusual for Rhonda and her boyfriend to leave for the casino after her work; they would arrive at the casino about 3 or 4 a.m. and they would gamble 8 or 10 hours each visit.

Her gambling trips escalated and she could justify the gambling because she received no pressure for grades or from family; to Rhonda, it was a perfect life.

When Rhonda turned 21, she was left $50,000 from a relative. She was still in University and doing well in school.

She continued gambling and was now playing Black Jack, Texas Hold Em as well as Roulette. The most she won was $6000 playing Texas Hold Em. When she won, she would put it back. The most she lost at an outing was $5200 playing Roulette. When she lost, she didn't feel badly as she felt 'energized' because she had an excuse to come back. She was now also betting with 'bookies' on NFL, college Football and Basketball games.

She became a casino Platinum Member (high-roller). This status awarded her free hotel rooms, free meals, limo pick-up for herself and boyfriend (she was never picked up from her home) gambling coupons, and other perks.

When she was 23 years old, her mother questioned her about gambling. Her father didn't believe there was a problem. Rhonda said it was just fun trips to the casino and not to worry. She was not a drinker and has never done drugs, but Rhonda knew she was addicted to gambling. She has never borrowed money from friends to gamble. She said gamblers do lie.

Turning 26 years old, the gambling escalated. It was not unusual for Rhonda and the boyfriend to spend two or three days at the casino. Her boyfriend would call in sick and her parents thought she was with her girlfriends on an out-of-town trip. These outings could result in losses from $1000 to $5000.

Rhonda began to experience major losses. In six years, Rhonda lost her inheritance of $50,000 and maxed her credit cards to the limit of $25,000 (three credit cards). She was not sleeping well, felt nervous and in her words 'just a wreck'. She finally told her parents that she needed help.

Rhonda's father agreed to pay off her credit card debt only if she would sign a contract not to set foot in another casino. He also monitored her whereabouts and wanted to know when and where she was going and with whom. When asked how she felt about signing the contract, she said she knew she had to sign it. She owed her father approximately $190,000 (her tuition, additional expensive tuition courses, and of course, her gambling debt). He does not want to be paid, just assured that she will not gamble.

Dealing with her withdrawal has not and is not easy. She said at times she felt resentful, bitter and bored. It wasn't fair; she felt she could control the gambling. She still feels drawn to the Casino, but of course, she is afraid to go. She had planned a trip to Las Vegas with girlfriends but the day before they were to leave, she backed out. She has not sought professional help.

Today, at 28 years old, Rhonda has completed a 4-yr. General B.A. and went on to complete her Master's degree. She wants to be a Criminal Analyst and has taken courses related to criminology, specializing in sexual predators.

Rhonda has moved to Edmonton where she has taken a contract position with a Medical Clinic. There are casinos in Edmonton. I wish her well and thank her for her disclosure of her addiction.

**DON'T JUDGE THOSE WHO TRY AND FAIL. JUDGE ONLY THOSE WHO FAIL TO TRY**

## Lil and Sam

I met and interviewed Lil and Sam, a delightful, elderly couple from Dundas, Ontario.

Lil and Sam are in their mid 70s, and have now been married 12 years. Both were married before and met while on vacation. Both retired in their 60s, had professional jobs, and retired comfortably. Sam does not drink, Lil enjoys an occasional drink and they both enjoy the odd cigarette when at the Casino.

Lil had been gambling for approximately 13 years. She was a slot player and quit gambling 3 years ago.

Sam was not a gambler before he married Lil. He had visited a couple of Casinos before he got married but only put in $20.00 each visit.

From the first time she visited a Casino, Lil enjoyed the atmosphere, the décor and sounds of a casino. She was fascinated and said that she felt she was entering a different world. What she enjoyed most was ordering a coffee, having a cigarette (when Canadian casinos permitted smoking) and sitting down at her favorite machine. Lil was not and is not a heavy smoker but she smoked the most when visiting a Casino.

Lil played the 25 cent slots and usually played the Blazing 7s; she always played 3 coins or 75 cents a pull; the machines now have buttons to push but still have the arm pull. The most she won in an outing was $1500 playing the 25 cent slots. The most she lost in an outing was $2000 playing the 25 cent slots.

Sam too, likes the excitement and atmosphere of the casino environment, and still gambles today.

The most Sam has won on an outing is $2400 and the most he has lost in an outing is $1000. He plays various machines and has played the $1.00 machines where he did win $1800. Today he will play the one cent, nickel, quarter and sometimes the dollar machines.

When asked how they spent their winnings, Lil said she put all her winnings back; if she won one day, the next day/visit, she would put it back. Sam did purchase some electronic equipment with one of his wins and an electric lawn mower with another win.

When they were gambling on a regular basis (3 or 4 times a week); it was not unusual to spend anywhere from 5 to 10 hours in the Casino. They would take breaks, have lunch, and on occasion take advantage of the overnight room 'comps'. The longest time they spent playing was 15 hours. She said she felt that gambling had consumed her.

When she won, she felt elated and wanted to play more because now she had money to play with. If she left a winner she felt ecstatic and was on top of the world. When she lost, she said she felt "stupid for spending the time and money at the Casino."

Sam, of course, loved it when he won (felt like "King of the World") and he still enjoys the Casino visits. When he loses, he says he "becomes quiet and subdued and sometimes withdrawn."

On one occasion when Lil won a Jackpot (approximately $350), she brought her coins home with her (at that time, payouts were issued in coin; payouts are now issued in paper form and the players can cash the 'slips' at the Cashier window or at the Ticket Redemption Machines located throughout the Casino). She sat her buckets of coins in the car and they spilled over under her feet. When her friend asked if she wanted to scoop them up; Lil said, "Oh No, just leave them, I like the feel of money under my feet." She drove home happily listening to the clinking of the coins under her feet!

Lil realized she had a problem and was addicted after an occasion, when at the casino, she waited for her favorite machine. In a row of the Blazing 7 machines, she saw that the Progressive Jackpot on this specific machine was approximately $530. She watched a man put in quite a bit of money; he finally left and did not hit the Jackpot. Lil eagerly sat down and began to play, thinking surely this machine would pay. She always played the maximum 3 quarters or 75 cents (one must play the max. to win the Progressive Jackpot. If you play 2 quarters and hit three 7s, you win $75, if you play the max. and hit three Blazing 7s, you win the Progressive Jackpot amount which is displayed on the top monitor of the machine). Lil put in $500 ($20 at a time), then went to the ATM and withdrew another $500 and put that in. She went to the ATM for the third time and withdrew another $500. All the time, the Jackpot is accumulating but she did not win! She played the last of her credits, looked at the displayed amount of the Jackpot, and then said to herself "Are you completely insane? Why have I spent $1500 to try to win a $540 plus Jackpot? What is wrong with me?" Lil got up, left the machine, and said "I will never play again." That was three years ago. Since that time, she has gambled on two occasions; on one visit she put a $20 bill half-way into a machine and then withdrew it. She said she felt sick. On another visit, she put $20 into a machine, won, then lost $60. She said she knew then it was over. The thrill and anticipation she had felt before was not there and she has not gambled since.

When asked how she felt about losing this much money, Lil said, "Sometimes I have regrets about the amount of money lost when it could have been spent on other things. However, the euphoria and good times compensated for the losses."

Lil also disclosed: "I felt like a closet gambler; as we did not, nor do we now discuss the Casino visits with the neighbors. Why would we – it is our money and of no business to our neighbors. I guess I wondered 'what will they think of me or us'. Just as a smoker trying to quit – there is guilt, or an alcoholic who hasn't admitted there is a problem, gambling too, comes with a stigma."

Lil or Sam never borrowed money to gamble. Over the years, Lil figures she has lost approximately $90,000 (from her savings) and Sam has lost over $35,000 (from his savings).

Sam feels that he is now in control of his gambling and limits his Casino visits because he realized the losses were too much and that he had to limit his spending on this form of entertainment. He now does not take any Debit or Credit cards for ATM access.

Lil and Sam still visit the Casinos today (Canadian and U.S.). Their visits are limited to once or twice a month. Lil does not gamble but enjoys the outings and doesn't mind going with Sam. Nor does she mind that Sam still gambles. She said, "It is his money and he enjoys the Casino, and I enjoy watching him playing." Sam takes $400 each visit and whether he wins or loses, that is his loss limit.

Lil has $100 tucked away in her purse, and said "just in case a machine beckons her"; as of this writing, she has not spent it gambling. She did say, "If Sam should die first, if I am able, I plan to take $1000 to the Casino and play my favorite Blazing 7s in honor of Sam."

**A Gambler is a Gambler, is a Gambler ……Until …..**

They continue to live comfortably in their own home, take winter vacations, enjoy life and are both healthy. That is the best win of all!

**IF YOU FIND A PATH WITH NO OBSTACLES, IT PROBABLY DOESN'T LEAD ANYWHERE**

TEXAS HOLD'EM
I ♥ THIS BAR & GRILL
B.B. KING'S BLUES CLUB
Hoover Dam
WELCOME TO Fabulous LAS VEGAS
NIAGARA FALLS
KANGAROOS – AUSTRALIA

♣ ♦ ♥ ♠

# CHAPTER 12
# TEXAS HOLD EM POKER

**TEXAS HOLD EM POKER**

Texas Hold Em Poker is extremely popular in Casinos internationally as well as on-line. Today there are 35 million registered players who play on-line, from 235 countries, and 1.8 million hands are played per hour. The websites are open 24/7 and attract young and older players. The Free-Play Tournaments have enticed many poker players who have won tournaments and then are invited to play in the Big Money Tournaments around the world (especially Las Vegas).

Texas Hold Em is a poker game played in a separate game room. Each table seats 9 (rarely played with more than 11 players) and the dealer. It is a 'community' card poker game played with one standard 52-card deck. Each Player is dealt a two-card hand (called *hole cards*), and that starts the first round of betting. Players can fold or hold at this point. The dealer then removes a card *(*burns a card*), and deals three more cards/community cards face-up (called *the flop*) in front of him on the table; players decide to hold or fold based on *the* flop, and now the second round of betting begins; the dealer burns another card and places the fourth card (called the *turn* card) beside his 3 cards, and the third round of betting begins, another card is *burned,* and then the last card is dealt (called the *river card*). The bets begin again and the best 5-card poker hand wins. The *flop* is the most important part of the hand. It is at this point that a player decides to stay and bet or fold. Many hands have been won/lost on the *river card*.

*Burning a card:* the dealer takes the top card from the deck because it could be marked and could be used to advantage of a player's hand.

**The Blinds**. The Limit and No- Limit game is always played with the Blind (the player who makes the first bet). He/she starts the game and each player must meet the ante; the player in the Blind also has the option of raising the bet when the action gets back to him/her.

**The Button** (looks like a small hockey puck) is placed in front of the last player who receives his/her cards last). The Button is moved from player to player after each pot.

Reference: Many books have been written on how to play the game. One of the poker world's greatest players, Doyle Brunson wrote a book called Super System (also titled: How I Made Over $1,000,000 Playing Poker) and he and his expert collaborators advises on when to bet, call, fold or raise. His last book, the 3$^{rd}$ edition had the 12$^{th}$ printing, and his monumental manual on how to win consistently at poker once sold for $100 (in 1978). Other editions were printed in 1979, 1984, 1989, 1994, and 2002 by B & G Publishing Company, Inc.

One of Doyle Brunson's famous quotes: "All you need is a chip and a chair."

Today, many poker players are writing books and sharing their theories and stories. One is Phil Hellmuth, also known as 'The Poker Brat' on the poker circuit. He has written several books and has his own official clothing line 'Poker Brat' business where funky, poker-designed T-shirts and other poker paraphernalia can be purchased. He has also won 11 World Series of Poker bracelets and is considered to be one of the best poker players in the Texas Hold Em game.

Daniel Negreanu, 37 years old, a Canadian, born in Toronto, is another professional poker player who, as of this writing, has won 4 World Series of Poker Bracelets, and 2 World Poker Tour Championships. He is currently ranked as 2$^{nd}$

on the all-time earnings list. He now makes his home in Las Vegas.

He too, is involved in charity events, e.g., "Ante Up For Africa". He is the founder of an annual "Big Swing" charity golf event, and makes many appearances to assist charities, as well as donating to them.

Daniel feels that some of his success at the tables is attributed to how he reads his opponents. He thinks the most important skill he employs is observing what hands his opponents play and how capable they are of playing them.

Many of the poker players are women and they too have won big in cash tournaments.

Annie Duke, for one, is an accomplished poker player, author, television personality, poker coach to the stars, a humanitarian, and a mother of four children. She is the winner of a World Series Poker bracelet. As well, she won a World Series of Poker Tournament in 2004, which makes her the top woman money winner in poker.

In 1994, with encouragement from her brother, Howard Lederer, also a famed poker-player, she entered a poker tournament in Las Vegas; she placed 13th in the tournament and knocked her brother Howard out of the tournament. She won $70,000 in her first month of competition.

At the time, she and her husband were living in Billings, CO. Shortly after, Annie and her husband moved to Las Vegas where she could play professionally.

In September, 2005, her autobiography <u>Annie Duke: How I Raised, Folded, Bluffed, Cursed and won Millions at the World Series of Poker</u> was available for sale.

In 2010, she won the NBC heads-up poker tournament by defeating Erik Seidel (a well-known male player) in the final round to become the first woman to capture this coveted title.

Annie appeared on an episode of Celebrity Apprentice where she came in second to the famed Joan Rivers. I personally think that Annie should have won the challenge because as the leader of her team, they raised a huge amount of money for a charity. She worked very hard and was able to encourage well-known poker players to donate large sums of money to support her on Celebrity Apprentice. Her team raised a huge amount of money (the most amount of all the other teams) which was donated to charity. Today, she is still very involved in fund-raisers for charity, and as well as holding her own fund-raisers, she is invited to many events as a Keynote speaker; the most recent was at the Women in Poker Hall of Fame Dinner.

She originally started out with the ambition to be a teacher. She holds a major in English and Psychology from Columbia University.

I wanted to include a poker player's story in this book and the following is Sharon's story which she was willing to share regarding her poker-playing and Casino experiences.

**Sharon's Story**

Sharon is 34 years old, single, and likes to play Texas Hold Em poker when visiting a casino. She used to play Blackjack but doesn't anymore. She occasionally will play the slots and has played the nickel slots but prefers the quarter slots. She visits once or twice a month on a regular basis if time permits (she has a job with flexible hours which allows her the casino visits).

The most she has lost was $2200 playing Blackjack. The most she has won playing poker is $2800 net. In one $2/$5 poker game, after game she had three buy-ins of $300 each or $900; when she was into her third buy-in of $300, she was down to $55 and ended up winning $2800.

She likes playing poker at Niagara Fallsview Casino. She feels comfortable playing there as she knows employees on staff and other regular players. She was invited and played in a tournament in Montreal and really liked the Poker Room as it had its own floor just for Poker; she said she found it was easier to concentrate and it had a very relaxed atmosphere.

She plays in games where the ante can be $1/$2, $2/$5, $5/$10 and no limit Texas Hold Em.

She has played in Cash Games and Tournaments but prefers the Cash Game.

The longest poker session she played in was for 36 hours (with breaks in between).

**Cash Games:**

**Advantages:**

There is no ante, blinds never go up, and the better poker hands are played.

You can leave when you wish.

**Disadvantages:**

Lower-stake games bring inexperienced players that get lucky and leave.

The payouts on average aren't as large as Tournament Poker.

You tend to risk more to win less.

**Tournament Playing:**

**Advantages:**

There are bigger payouts with less investment.

**Disadvantages:**

Only the few top players/winners (depending on structure of tournament) make money.

Antes and blinds tend to go up quickly forcing one to play hands that normally might not have been played (more luck involved).

When asked if she ever felt she was addicted, she explained that "at times when it's not going well, try to stay and win back losses, and or exceed intended amount to be spent."

Sharon sets a limit when she visits a casino; she sticks to her limit 90% of the time and has never borrowed money to gamble.

The perks she has received at Casinos include meals, cigarettes, rooms and show tickets.

Other Comments from Sharon:

"Gambling life is completely its own style of living; the rush one gets when winning/losing cannot be explained. The competitiveness in Poker is like no other game I've played (it can get personal at times; especially as a female)."

Other: She did witness a well-known 34-yr. old circuit poker player (he plays in the TV series "Poker After Dark") lose 1.2 million dollars in an hour and a half playing Roulette in a Montreal casino.

**POKER TIPS**

1. Do Not Play Every Hand/Learn to Fold

Playing more hands does not lead to winning more money; it usually means losing more.

2. Do Not Over-Drink When Playing

You may feel more relaxed after one or two drinks, but this habit can lead to you becoming a "loser" and not as sharp and you start playing carelessly, causing losses.

3. Do Not Bluff for The Sake of Bluffing

Bluffing is part of the game, but it is better to never bluff than "just to bluff"; it can cost you.

Unless you are familiar with how a player/players play the game.

It can work but also can backfire.

4. Do Not Stay in a Hand Just Because You are Already in It

Don't chase your money - just because you have put "that much in the pot".

If you are pretty sure another player has the best hand – FOLD.

5. Do Not Stay for the River Card to "Keep Someone Honest"

Do not 'call' just to see if his/her cards really are/were better than your hand.

6. Do Not Play If You Are Not Really In The Right Frame of Mind

If you are upset or in a bad mood, do not play and use this as an excuse to escape from the personal issues or if you are "having a bad day".

Never Play on Tilt, e.g., playing emotionally NOT rationally can cost you; fellow players can/will sense your mood and take advantage of your lack of concentration/frustration.

7. Pay Attention to the Cards on the Table

Figure out what the best possible hand could be to fill the "Flop"; make sure you notice Flush or Straight possibilities.

Pay attention to what is showing and who has folded with what was showing.

8. Pay Attention to Other Players

Observe your opponents even when you are not in the hand.

Becoming familiar with their style of play can help you, e.g., follows:

(Once you know that the number 4 player always folds to a re-raise on the River Card, there is a possible chance that you can bluff and take down a pot).

9. Do not play 'over your limit' Games

Do not play at stakes that make you think about the actual money in terms of day-to-day life OR with money you cannot afford to lose.

Even if you had one super good night of winning at $2/$4, resist the urge to play at $5/$10 stakes.

10. Do Pick the Right Game for Your Skill Level and Bankroll

Do not jump into a $5/$10 just because you won a huge amount at $2//$4; the higher the limit, the more you can lose

You want to be the best, not the "Fish" sitting in with the "Sharks".

If you are winning money at low level games, why change – You Are Winning!

"All-in can make or break you".

Poker is a mind game and knowing when to change gears.

Note: A big part of this game is having the money to raise and having the nerve to "bluff" to force your opponents to fold. Money management plays a big part as well.

**Job Position: Poker Dealer**

**Las Vegas**

I met Julie, a Texas Hold Em Poker dealer in a casino in Las Vegas. Julie has been a dealer for over 25 years dealing various table and poker games, i.e., Omaha/Top Limit/ High/Low Split, as well as many big-money tournaments.

Julie was a very attractive 69 year- old but looked about 50 (no surgery either; I asked). She has dealt to the big-money circuit players and the one thing that she doesn't like about her job is when players are rude. Of all the players who have sat at her table, she did say that Dan Negreanu, the Cdn. player was the most respectful of the women dealers.

She has worked the night shift (3 a.m. to 11 a.m. or swing shift from 1 a.m. to 9 a.m.) for 30 years and loves these shifts. The money is good; she loves her job and loves living in Las Vegas. She gambles, but most of her gambling is done off the strip, at the smaller casinos.

Note: The Texas Hold Em Dealers are allowed to keep their own tips; they do not have to be shared.

**TEXAS HOLD EM TOURNAMENTS FOR CHARITIES**

Many clubs and organizations hold these fund-raising tournaments in support of various charities or for revenue to support their own needs. i.e., our grandchildren are Irish Dancers and their dance school, The Raeany School of Dance, Hamilton, ON, has held fund-raising tournaments to support the dancers and help subsidize the out-of-town competitions in Canada and the U.S.

Note: I have never played Texas Hold Em Poker; however, was allowed into a Poker Room to see a tournament in progress. The TV Poker Channel draws many viewers for Texas Hold Em Poker; this is a spectator's sport!

**TEXAS HOLD EM BONUS POKER**

This is a new game that casinos are offering. Texas Hold Em Bonus Poker is a community card poker game different from the traditional Texas Hold Em played in poker rooms. The object of the game, for Player and Dealer alike, is to make the best five-card poker hand using any combination from their two-card hand and the five-community cards/board cards. There is no Player-to Player competition; Players compare their hands to the Dealer's hand.

This game is played "heads-up" meaning each Player plays against the Dealer, and the best poker hand wins. For this reason, all wagers (Ante, Bonus, Flop, Turn and River), are made before the Player views the cards, each step of the way.

There is also an optional side bet "Bonus Jackpot" wager where players compare their two-card hand to the posted pay table. Players need not win in the base game to be paid on the bonus wager, provided the side bet wager was placed prior to any cards being dealt and the Player's two-card hand matched one of the payout hands.

**Note:** Poker players are always coming up with new games and, if they prove to be good games, they are presented to Management and if approved by the Gaming Commission or game regulators, they will eventually show up in the Casinos.

**Big Money** – A table dealer did tell me that to play with the big players, you need big money, e.g., at least $10,000 - $15,000 if you want to get into the big money tournament poker games.

♣ ♦ ♥ ♠

# CHAPTER 13
# HOW BIG IS THE INDUSTRY?

## HOW BIG IS THE INDUSTRY?

Just how big is the gaming industry? According to a news report in the *Hamilton Spectator*, June 11, 2011, Asia will be home to the world's two biggest casino markets as early as this year, with Singapore set to take the No. 2 spot from Las Vegas, a US gambling industry group said.

Frank Fahrenkopf, president of the American Gaming Association, said Singapore raked in $5.1 billion US in gaming revenue last year and could bring in up to US$6.4 billion this year.

In 2006, Macau beat out Las Vegas for the No. 1 spot for gambling, with earnings of US$5.8 billion in casino revenue. The prediction is that revenue in Macau will probably grow 25% to 50% this year.

However, Macau faces several problems that could affect this growth, including a labor shortage and the lack of infrastructure as well as the government cap on the number of new gambling tables, until 2013.

There are 400,000 people employed in the gaming industry in the US. These are huge numbers and account for a lot of jobs.

## CASINOS IN CANADA

Over the past three decades, the Great Canadian Gaming Corporation has become one of Canada's leading providers for entertainment.

The number of Casinos in the Provinces in Canada:

- Alberta (29)
- British Columbia (21)
- Manitoba (16)
- Newfoundland and Labrador (1)
- Nova Scotia (7)
- Ontario (30)
- Prince Edward Island (2)
- Quebec (11)
- Saskatchewan (11)

- Yukon Territory (1)

**ONTARIO CASINOS/RACEWAYS/SLOTS**

Ajax Downs

Brantford Casino

Campbellville

Clinton Raceway

Dresden

Flamboro Downs

Fort Erie Racetrack

Gananoque

Georgian Downs Raceway

Grand River Raceway

Hanover Raceway

Hiawatha Horse Park

Kawartha Downs

Kenora

London

Mohawk Racetrack

Niagara Falls Casino

Niagara Fallsview

Orillia (Casino Rama)

Peterborough

Point Edward

Port Perry (Great Blue Heron Casino)

Rideau Carleton Raceway

Sarnia

Sault Ste. Marie Casino

Sudbury Downs

Thousand Islands Casino

Thunder Bay Casino

Western Fair District

Woodbine Racetrack

Reported in *The Hamilton Spectator, Nov. 23, 2011* - Hamilton-Niagara's Top Employers 2012.

Niagara Fallsview Casino Resort was named as one of the top 10 Employers in the Hamilton-Niagara region.

Now entering its sixth year, Hamilton-Niagara's Top Employers is an annual competition organized by the editors of Canada's Top 100 Employers. This special designation recognizes the employers in the Hamilton-Niagara area of Ontario that lead their industries in offering exceptional places to work.

The editors examined the recruitment histories of more than 75,000 employers across Canada that it tracks for its popular job search site, Eluta.ca. From this initial group, editors invited 10,000 of the fastest-growing employers to apply, plus another 2,500 companies and organizations in industries that they wanted to examine more closely. Employers completed an extensive application process that included a detailed review of their operations and Human Resource practices.

Selection Process

Employers are evaluated by the editors of Canada's Top 100 Employers using the same eight criteria as the national competition:

◊ Community Involvement

◊ Employee Communication

◊ Health, Financial and Family Benefits

◊ Performance Management

◊ Physical Workplace

◊ Training and Skills Development

◊ Vacation and Time Off

◊ Work/Social Atmosphere

Employers are compared to other organizations in their field to determine which offer the most progressive and forward-thinking programs.

"Recognized as a corporate leader, we also give back to the community through a variety of civic leadership and charitable initiatives. Through our *Green Initiative*, we've made amazing progress in adopting sustainable business practices to lessen our operational impact on the environment."

*The Niagara Fallsview Casino employs 2749 full-time employees. They offer a number of great financial benefits, including year-end performance bonuses, generous employee discounts on its products, discounted financial services through a group banking program and matching Registered Savings Plan contributions.

For information on employment opportunities, visit: niagaracasinosjobs.com

**Ontario Lottery & Gaming Commission**

In June, 2011, the Ontario Lottery & Gaming Corporation gave over $2 billion in gambling revenue to the Province of Ontario. This revenue gift is a huge boost for the coffers of many communities and will, of course, benefit many. This money contribution is to be used to support Ontario's hospitals, schools, amateur sports, culture, and charities. As well, the Ontario Lotto and Gaming Corporation will pay out $11.6 million in one-time 'pay-for-performance' bonuses to approximately 6,000 employees. This too, is a positive side to the sharing of the wealth. Gamblers, who are reading this, can at least feel that they have helped with this contribution!

Reported in the Hamilton Spectator:

As of January, 2012, the City of Hamilton, Ontario has received more than 49.9 million of non-taxed gaming revenue from the Slots at Flamboro Downs Casino since it opened in October 2000. This revenue assists with many Hamilton and surrounding area community projects.

**Comment:** As a resident of Hamilton, I would really like to see how that money has been used as we never really hear or read about it in the media and our residential taxes never go down; they always increase on an annual basis.

Fact: In 2010, the Ontario Lottery and Gaming Commission brought in $1.9 billion to the treasury of the Province of Ontario.

The Great Canadian Gaming Corporation is one of Canada's leading providers of entertainment. They have casinos in 17 locations in the following provinces and Washington State:

**British Columbia**

Boulevard Casino

Casino Nanaimo

Chances Dawson Creek

Chilliwack Bingo

Fraser Downs Racetrack & Casino

Hastings Racecourse

Maple Ridge Community Gaming Centre

River Rock Casino Resort

View Royal Casino

**Nova Scotia**

Casino Nova Scotia Halifax

Casino Nova Scotia Sydney

**Ontario**

Flamboro Downs

Georgian Downs

**Note:** Any individual or Company who wishes to provide products or services in Canadian casinos must be registered. Different registrations apply based on gaming-related versus non-gaming-related applications. Application Fees are $200 but one can apply for exemption based on the type of application. Background checks are required and are thorough and include past employment records, financial statements and other important but pertinent information.

For gaming information see the Gaming Control Board website. This is a government agency charged with regulating casino and other types of gaming in a defined geographical area, usually a state, and of enforcing gaming law in general. The official name of the regulatory body varies among jurisdictions.

**The number of Casinos in the U.S.A.:**

- Alabama (7)
- Alaska (7)
- Arizona (37)
- Arkansas (3)
- California (182)
- Colorado (39)
- Connecticut (3)

- Delaware (4)
- Florida (140)
- Georgia (2)
- Idaho (16)
- Illinois (17)
- Indiana (13)
- Iowa (21)
- Kansas (8)
- Kentucky (8)
- Louisiana (45)
- Maine (13)
- Maryland (6)
- Massachusetts (2)
- Michigan (28)
- Minnesota (39)
- Mississippi (32)
- Missouri (13)
- Montana (143)
- Nebraska (11)
- Nevada (360)
- New Hampshire (3)
- New Jersey (15)
- New Mexico (29)
- New York (21)
- North Carolina (2)
- North Dakota (35)
- Ohio (8)
- Oklahoma (114)
- Oregon (15)
- Pennsylvania (10)
- Rhode Island (2)
- South Carolina (3)
- South Dakota (50)
- Texas (7)
- Virginia (1)
- Washington (125)
- West Virginia (5)
- Wisconsin (28)
- Wyoming (4)

**United States**

Great American Casino – Everett

Great American Casino – Kent

Great American Casino – Lakewood

Great American Casino – Tukwila

Note: Native American Casinos are subject to the provisions of the Indian Gaming Regulatory Act which is enforced by the Native Indian Gaming Commission (NIGC). The NIGC does not have jurisdiction over State-regulated casinos.

Over 54 million dollars was spent on lottery tickets in the U.S. in 2010.

Update:

December, 2011

The Province of Ontario's lottery agency has sent out requests for proposals seeking help to set up and run online gaming starting sometime in 2012. The Ontario Lottery and Gaming Corporation plans to phase in online gambling starting with casino-style games such as video poker and video slots along with online sales of lottery tickets.

♣ ♦ ♥ ♠

# CHAPTER 14
# GAMBLERS ANONYMOUS

**GAMBLERS ANONYMOUS**

**HISTORY**

The fellowship of Gamblers Anonymous is the outgrowth of a chance meeting between two men during the month of January in 1957. These men had a truly baffling history of trouble and misery due to an obsession to gamble. They began to meet regularly and as the months passed neither had returned to gambling.

They concluded from their discussions that in order to prevent a relapse it was necessary to bring about certain character changes within themselves. In order to accomplish this, they used for a guide certain spiritual principles which had been utilized by thousands of people who were recovering from other compulsive addictions. The word spiritual can be said to describe those characteristics of the human mind that represent the highest and finest qualities such as kindness, generosity, honesty and humility. Also, in order to maintain their own abstinence they felt that it was vitally important that they carry the message of hope to other compulsive gamblers.

As a result of favorable publicity by a prominent newspaper columnist and TV commentator, the first group meeting of Gamblers Anonymous was held on Friday, September 13, 1957, in Los Angeles, California. Since that time, the fellowship has grown steadily and groups are flourishing throughout the world.

## THE RECOVERY PROGRAM

### Steps for a Program of Recovery

1. We admitted we were powerless over gambling – that our lives had become unmanageable.

2. Came to believe that a Power greater than ourselves could restore us to a normal way of thinking and living.

3. Made a decision to turn our will and our lives over to the care of this Power of our own understanding.

4. Made a searching and fearless moral and financial inventory of ourselves.

5. Admitted to ourselves and to another human being the exact nature of our wrongs.

6. Were entirely ready to have these defects of character removed.

7. Humbly asked God (of our understanding) to remove our shortcomings.

8. Made a list of all persons we had harmed and became willing to make amends to them all.

9. Make direct amends to such people wherever possible, except when to do so would injure them or others.

10. Continued to take personal inventory and when we were wrong, promptly admitted it.

11. Sought through prayer and meditation to improve our conscious contact with God as we understood Him, praying only for knowledge of His will for us and the power to carry that out.

12. Having made an effort to practice these principles in all our affairs, we tried to carry this message to other compulsive gamblers.

The **12- Step Program** is fundamentally based on ancient spiritual principles and rooted in sound medical therapy.

The best recommendation for the program is the fact that "it works."

Gamblers Anonymous would like to indicate that we are not soliciting members. Our intention is to highlight that gambling for certain individuals is an illness called "*compulsive gambling.*" Gamblers Anonymous provides the message that there is an alternative to the destruction of compulsive gambling and this alternative is the Gamblers Anonymous program.

Our ranks are filled with members who have recovered from the illness by stopping gambling and attaining a normal way of life. These members remain ready to help any individual who passes through the Gamblers Anonymous door.

**QUESTIONS AND ANSWERS about the Problem of Compulsive Gambling and the Gambling Anonymous Recovery Program**

**What is compulsive gambling?**

The explanation that seems most acceptable to Gamblers Anonymous members is that compulsive gambling is an illness, progressive in its nature, which can never be cured, but can be arrested. Before coming to Gamblers Anonymous, many compulsive gamblers thought of themselves as morally weak or at times just plain 'no good'. The Gamblers Anonymous concept is that compulsive gamblers are really very sick people who can recover if they will follow to the best of their ability a simple program that has proved successful for thousands of other men and women with a gambling or compulsive gambling problem.

**What is the first thing a compulsive gambler ought to do in order to stop gambling?**

The compulsive gambler needs to be willing to accept the fact that he or she is in the grip of a progressive illness and has a desire to get well. Our experience has shown that the Gamblers Anonymous program will always work for any person who has a desire to stop gambling. However, it will never work for the person who will not face squarely the facts about the illness.

**How can you tell whether you are a compulsive gambler?**

Only you can make that decision. Most people turn to Gamblers Anonymous when they become willing to admit that gambling has them licked. Also in Gamblers Anonymous, a compulsive gambler is described as a person whose gambling has caused growing and continuing problems in any department of his or her life.

Many Gamblers Anonymous members went through terrifying experiences before they were ready to accept help. Others were faced with a slow, subtle deterioration which finally brought them to the point of admitting defeat.

**Can a compulsive gamblers ever gamble normally again?**

No. The first bet to a problem gambler is like the first small drink to an alcoholic. Sooner or later he or she falls back into the same old destructive pattern.

Once a person has crossed the invisible line into irresponsible uncontrolled gambling he or she never seems to regain control. After abstaining a few months some of our members have tried some small bet experimentation, always with disastrous results. The old obsession inevitably returned.

Our Gamblers Anonymous experience seems to point to these alternatives: to gamble, risking progressive deterioration or not to gamble, and develop a better way of life.

**Why can't a compulsive gambler simply use will power to stop gambling?**

We believe that most people, if they are honest, will recognize their lack of power to solve certain problems. When it comes to gambling, we have known many problem gamblers who could abstain for long stretches, but caught off guard and under the right set of circumstances, they started gambling without thought of the consequences. The defenses they relied upon, through will power alone, gave way before some trivial reason for placing a bet. We have found that will power and self-knowledge will not help in those mental blank spots, but adherence to spiritual principles seems to solve our problems. Most of us feel that a belief in Power greater than ourselves is necessary in order for us to sustain a desire to refrain from gambling.

**Do Gamblers Anonymous members go into gambling places to help former members who are still gambling?**

No. Families and friends of these people have asked us to intercede but we have never been able to be of any real help. Actually, sometimes we felt we retarded a member's eventual recovery by giving them this unsolicited attention. It all goes back to the basic principle that a gambler ought to want help before he or she is approached by us.

**I only go on gambling binges periodically. Do I need Gamblers Anonymous?**

Yes. Compulsive gamblers who have joined Gamblers Anonymous tell us that, though their gambling binges were periodic, the intervals between were not periods of constructive thinking. Symptomatic of these periods were nervousness, irritability, frustration, indecision and a continued breakdown in personal relationships. These same people have often found the Gamblers Anonymous program the answer to the elimination of character defects and a guide to moral progress in their lives.

**GAMBLING, for the compulsive gambler is defined as follows:**

**Any betting or wagering, for self or others, whether for money or not, no matter how slight or insignificant, where the outcome is uncertain or depends upon chance or 'skill' constitutes gambling.**

**If I join Gamblers Anonymous won't everyone know I am a compulsive gambler?**

Most people made quite a name for themselves as full-fledged-gamblers by the time they turned to Gamblers

Anonymous. Their gambling was not usually a well-kept secret. It would then be unusual if the good news of their abstinence from gambling did not cause comment. However, no disclosure of any affiliation with Gamblers Anonymous can rightfully be made by anyone but the member themselves. Even then, it should be done in such a way that will work no hardship on the Gamblers Anonymous fellowship.

**If I stop gambling won't it make it difficult for me to keep some desirable business and social contacts?**

We think not. Most of the world's work of any consequence is done without the benefit of monetary wagering. Many of our leaders in business, industry and professional life have attained great success without knowing one card from another or which way the horses run around the track. In the area of social relationships, the newcomer will soon find a keen appreciation of the many pleasant and stimulating activities available – far removed from anything that is remotely associated from gambling.

**How does someone stop gambling through the Gamblers Anonymous program?**

One does this through bringing about a progressive character change within oneself. This can be accomplished by having faith in – and following – the basic concepts of the Gamblers Anonymous Recovery Program.

There are no short cuts in gaining this faith and understanding. To recover from one of the most baffling, insidious, compulsive addictions will require diligent effort. HONESTY, OPENMINDEDNESS AND WILLINGNESS are the key words used in our recovery.

**Can a person recover by himself/herself by reading Gamblers Anonymous literature or medical books on the problem of compulsive gambling?**

Sometimes, but not usually. The Gamblers Anonymous program works best for the individual when it is recognized and accepted as a program involving other people. Working with other compulsive gamblers in a Gamblers Anonymous group the individual seems to find the necessary understanding and support. They are able to talk of their past experiences and present problems in an area where they are comfortable and accepted. Instead of feeling alone and misunderstood, they feel needed and accepted.

**Does Gamblers Anonymous look upon compulsive gambling as a vice?**

No.

**Is knowing why we gambled important?**

Perhaps, however insofar as stopping gambling, many Gamblers Anonymous members have abstained from gambling without the knowledge of why they gambled.

**What are some characteristics of a person who is a compulsive gambler?**

1. INABILITY AND UNWILLINGNESS TO ACCEPT REALITY. Hence the escape into into the dream world of gambling.

2. EMOTIONAL INSECURITY. A compulsive gambler finds he or she is emotionally comfortable only when "in action". It is not uncommon to hear a Gambler Anonymous member say: "The only place I really felt like I belonged was sitting at the poker table. There I felt secure and comfortable. No great demands were made upon me. I knew I was destroying myself, yet at the same time, I had a certain sense of security."

3. IMMATURITY. A desire to have all the good things in life without any great effort on their part seems to be the common character pattern of problem gamblers. Many Gamblers Anonymous members accept the fact that they were unwilling to grow up. Subconsciously they felt they could avoid mature responsibility by wagering on the spin of a wheel or the turn of a card, and so the struggle to escape responsibility finally became a subconscious obsession.

Also, a compulsive gambler seems to have a strong inner urge to be a 'big shot' and needs to have a feeling of being all powerful. The compulsive gambler is willing to do anything (often of an antisocial nature) to maintain the image he or she wants others to see.

Then too, there is a theory that compulsive gamblers subconsciously want to lose to punish themselves. There is much evidence to support this theory.

**What is the dream world of the compulsive gambler?**

This is another common characteristic of compulsive gamblers. A lot of the time is spent creating images mages of the great and wonderful things they are going to do as soon as they make the big win. They often see themselves as quite philanthropic and charming people. They may dream of providing families and friends with news cars, mink coats, and other luxuries. Compulsive gamblers picture themselves leading a pleasant gracious life, made possible by the huge sums of money they will accrue from their 'system'. Servants, penthouses, nice clothes, charming friends, yachts, and world tours are a few of the wonderful things that are just around the corner after a big win if finally made.

Pathetically, however, there never seems to be a big enough winning to make even the smallest dream come true. When compulsive gamblers succeed, they gamble to dream still greater dreams. When failing, they gamble in reckless desperation and the depths of their misery are fathomless as their dream world comes crashing down. Sadly, they will struggle back, dream more dreams, and of course suffer more misery. No one can convince them that their great schemes will not someday come true. They believe they will, for without this dream world, life for them would not be tolerable.

**Isn't compulsive gambling basically a financial problem?**

No, compulsive gambling is an emotional problem. A person in the grip of this illness creates mountains of apparently insolvable problems. Of course, financial problems are created, but they also find themselves facing marital, employment, or legal problems. Compulsive gamblers find friends have been lost and relatives have rejected them. Of the many serious difficulties created, the financial problems seem the easiest to solve. When a compulsive gambler enters Gamblers Anonymous and quits gambling, income is usually increased and there is no longer the financial drain that was caused by gambling, and very shortly, the financial pressure begins to be relieved. Gamblers Anonymous members have found that the best road to financial recovery is through hard work and repayment of our debts. Bankruptcy, borrowing and/or lending of money (bailouts) in Gamblers is detrimental to our recovery and should not take place.

The most difficult and time consuming problem with which they will be faced is that of bringing a character change within themselves. Most Gamblers Anonymous members look upon this as their greatest challenge, which should be worked on immediately and continued throughout their lives.

**Who can join Gamblers Anonymous?**

Anyone who has a desire to stop gambling. There are no other rules or regulations concerning Gamblers Anonymous membership.

**How much does it cost to join Gamblers Anonymous?**

There are no assessments in connection with Gamblers Anonymous membership. The newcomer signs nothing and pledges nothing. However, we do have expenses relative to our group meeting and our Gambler Anonymous service facilities. Since Gamblers Anonymous has traditionally been fully self supporting and declines outside contribution, these expenses are met through voluntary financial support by the members. Experience has shown that acceptance of these financial responsibilities is a vital part of our individual and group growth process.

**Why are Gamblers Anonymous members anonymous?**

Anonymity has great practical value in maintaining unity within our fellowship. Through its practice at the level of press, radio, films and television, we have eliminated the possibility of fame and recognition being given to the individual member; hence, we have not been faced with any great internal struggles for power and prestige which would prove highly detrimental to our essential unity.

Anonymity also has great value in attracting new members who initially might feel there is a stigma attached to the problem. Therefore, we guarantee the newcomer as much anonymity as they choose.

More importantly, we are beginning to realize that anonymity has tremendous spiritual significance. It represents a powerful reminder that we need always place principles above personalities.

Our survival as individuals, demands that we renounce personal gratification . . . so our Gamblers Anonymous movement not only advocates but tries to practice true humility and it is through greater humility that we will be able to live in peace and security for all the years to come.

### Is Gamblers Anonymous a religious society?

No. Gamblers Anonymous is composed of people from many religious faiths along with agnostics and atheists. Since membership in Gamblers Anonymous requires no particular religious belief as a condition of membership, it cannot be described as a religious society. The Gamblers Anonymous recovery program is based on acceptance of certain spiritual values but the member is free to interpret these principles as he chooses.

**Note:** When I contacted Gamblers Anonymous to request permission to print their material in this book, a very pleasant man named Dave answered my call. He advised that "permission is not required to print their material as the more information out there about Gamblers Anonymous the better."

**MANY TIMES IT REQUIRES MORE STRENGTH DECIDING WHAT TO DO THAN IT DOES PERFORMING THE TASK**

## PROBLEM GAMBLING – When help is needed – Get the needed help!

If you are a spouse, family member or friend with a gambling problem, it is natural to want to help. However, they may not be ready, or willing, to admit that there is a problem. While gambling may be negatively affecting you and your family, you cannot force someone to stop. Before raising the issue, you can:

◊ Get informed – understand the problem first. Research problem gambling on websites like

www.responsiblegambling.org

◊ Be prepared – if there is a chance of violent behavior, exercise caution. Get a support system in place – family, friends, clergy or counselor

◊ Choose the right moment – if the person is expressing remorse about gambling, or has just finished a gambling episode, this could be a good time to talk

Raising your concerns:

◊ Use an "I" point of view: Express feelings with "I feel" or "I think." The listener will feel less defensive and an argument will be less likely

◊ Remain calm – keep a cool head when talking about the person's gambling and other hot-button issues like family finances

◊ Negotiate and set firm boundaries – make clear your expectations about future gambling, managing finances and responsibilities.

Support

◊ Recognize and acknowledge positive steps and give praise for successes

◊ A counselor or a self-help group can help you to communicate effectively, reduce the guilt and raise self-esteem

◊ Change takes time; it may take several tries before the person successfully changes their gambling behavior.

## THE BEST ANGLE TO APPROACH ANY PROBLEM IS THE TRY-ANGLE

From the New York Council on Problem Gambling, Inc.

More than three-quarter million adult residents have experienced problems due to gambling at some point during their lifetime. In New York State, between 1986 and 1996, the prevalence of problem gambling rose by 74%.

Problem gamblers are individuals who experience difficulties due to gambling but who do not meet the diagnostic criteria for pathological gambling at this time.

Pathological (compulsive) gambling is defined as an "impulse control disorder" in the Diagnostic and Statistical Manual (DSM-IV) of the American Psychiatric Association, characterized by a progressive, uncontrollable urge to gamble.

Problem or pathological gambling is known as a "hidden" disorder, as there are no visible symptoms associated with the illness, leaving its victims appearing normal long after their lives are affected.

**Hope for You and Yours - Problem Gambling 24-Hour Helpline: 1-800-437-1611**

www.nyproblemgambling.org
council@nyproblemgambling.org

**Statements I Have Heard from Gamblers:**

"I become a different person when I enter a casino."

"I tend to enter another mind-zone when it comes to gambling."

"I'm like a kid in a candy store when I get into a casino" (that would be me).

**A FORM OF DENIAL/REALLY!** Statements I have heard while writing this book:

◊ I don't gamble, but bet my friend $5.00 that . . .!

◊ I don't gamble, but play on-line games for points (which you must buy for cash)!

◊ I don't gamble; I just play the tables!

◊ I don't gamble, but I do go to the track once in awhile and bet a few races!

◊ I don't gamble, but I do play Texas Hold Em on-line!

◊ I don't gamble, but we play Poker every two weeks and we put in $20 each!

◊ I don't gamble, but when on a cruise, I like to play $5.00 Blackjack!

◊ I don't gamble, but signed up for a Texas Hold Em Tournament at the Casino!

◊ I don't gamble, but like to go on the bus rides to the Casino!

◊ I don't gamble, but am going on the 3-day Casino bus tour because I like to shop!

◊ I don't gamble; I play the Stock Market!

◊ We don't gamble; we just go to the Casino/s to eat!

◊ I don't gamble, but always go into the football pools!

◊ I don't gamble but only buy lottery or scratch and win tickets!

◊ I don't gamble, but when I win, I always buy something with my winnings!

◊ I don't gamble but love going to Las Vegas!

◊ I don't gamble but like to play Keno!

◊ I don't gamble but when I go to the Casino, I only lose $20!

◊ I don't really gamble, but once in awhile I take off for the Casino on my own!

◊ I don't gamble, but sometimes play ProLine?

◊ I don't gamble but do go into monthly Card tournaments where we play for money!

**What can I say; you never know until you have been there, what you will hear people say!**

**Life is like a coin - you can spend it anyway you wish - but you can only spend it once.**

**A Major Concern:**

I personally feel that young children are being enticed for gambling; as an example, when our grandson was a 5-year-old, he was addicted to the Nintendo game, and it had to be taken from him. I have heard many similar stories from parents, teachers and grandparents.

Electronic gaming has a huge market and is targeted for children; the more gaming for children, the more chance of addiction. Children who are 'glued' to an electronic game do not have the same interaction as with 'real' people. Are children's' social skills being affected? Are their reading skills deteriorating?

Bullying has become a major problem in schools around the globe. There are games on the market that involve intense character-violence. Question: Could this type of game-addiction be one of the factors attributed to bullying? I think this is an area that needs to be continually studied.

As reported in *The Hamilton Spectator*, January 11, 2011, an article written by Lauren La Rose, *The Canadian Press* in her article titled *Problem Gaming Leads to Other Woes*:

Young problem gamers who play compulsively on their consoles and computers may be at greater risk than others for mental-health issues such as anxiety and depression.

In a two-year study, lead author Douglas Gentile, an associate professor of psychology at Iowa State University, was partners with researchers in Hong Kong and Singapore. They studied the game playing habits of over 3000 Singapore students in Grades 3, 4, 7, and 8.

The study included assessment of pathological gaming, weekly amount of game play, impulsiveness, social competence, depression, social phobia, anxiety and depression. In the study, published online and in the February issue of Pediatrics, researchers wrote that while game playing itself is not pathological in the beginning, it can become so for some individuals "when the activity becomes dysfunctional , harming the individual's social, occupational, family, school and psychological function."

In earlier research, Gentile said kids who were pathological gamers showed similar patterns with other variables seen in addictions like those to drugs and gambling. They tended to be male, have more hostile personalities, engage in more anti-social and aggressive behaviors and had worse grades in school.

Gentile said while they can't say conclusively pathological gaming is a casual link for mental health issues; it appears these problems tended to follow when kids became "addicted." Also, "What we should be teaching kids is how to put it back into balance: that they need to be able to prioritize, make sure their homework gets done first, that they're spending good time with their family and friends."

Limits should be set on how much time their kids sit in front of TV and video game screens as well as limits on content so it is age appropriate; that's "a powerful protector factor for kids."

There are so many young people who go to the casinos today. Are they spending their hard-earned money or tuition money recklessly? Student-debt is also a concern today (too much money borrowed for education? Or being used for gambling)? These are legitimate questions and cause for concern. Many pensioners are spending their retirement funds and can get hurt financially.

Note: From what I have seen and been told by casino personnel:

"More women play the slots than men. More men play the table games."

My parents advised me years ago not to marry a drinker or a gambler; I didn't. Are mother's today advising their sons not to marry a woman who gambles? Good question.

**FAMILY CASINO VISITS**

What I have observed on casino visits is the number of families who bring their children. While children are not allowed in the casino gaming areas, they are allowed in the pool and recreation areas provided. They are allowed to go from point A to point B through the casino but must be with a parent and are escorted through the casino with security personnel, e.g., from the Lobby to the restaurants or shopping areas.

**The family who plays together stays together!**

**CONCLUSION**

As stated in the beginning, this book was not written to promote gambling. Nor was it written for me to make a lot of money. A fact is there is not a lot of money to be made in the self-publishing industry unless you write a best-seller. This whole endeavor was based on encouragement from family and friends, as well as the journals that I kept on my personal travels to the various casinos, and the adventures and fun experienced getting there and being there.

The people I met and their willingness to share information about themselves and their jobs in the casinos also was also a motivator.

I wanted to write about the positive side to give an idea of the number of jobs created and available in this rapidly growing world-wide industry. How casinos and their personnel contribute to their communities for very worthwhile causes is encouraging as the general public never really hears about the positive aspect of the gaming industry.

I still gamble occasionally and continue to enjoy this as a form of entertainment; I also respect the form that it is, and leave when I'm losing. As the well-known country song goes, "You got to know when to hold 'em, know when to fold 'em, know when to walk away and know when to run'…"

Remember: You do not go to a casino to get rich.

For the compulsive gamblers who need or wish help, I quote from the Gamblers Anonymous Recovery Program: **"To recover from one of the most baffling, insidious, compulsive addictions will require diligent effort. Honesty, Open-mindedness, and Willingness are the key words in our recovery."**

I have always kept notes/journals of travels, experiences, etc., and decided 2 years ago that I wanted to put it in a book. This pot pourri of gambling-related stories and events, as well as a bit of history has finally come to be in book-form, and again I thank everyone who was involved in helping this come to fruition.

I hope you enjoyed the read!

**THE REAL SECRET OF HAPPINESS IS NOT WHAT YOU GIVE OR WHAT YOU RECEIVE - IT IS WHAT YOU SHARE**

## ACKNOWLEDGEMENTS

Special thanks to Summer Ramsamy, Friesen Press, who answered all my questions before I decided to go with this publisher. Caroline Shaw, my Account Manager, was absolutely marvelous with her assistance and excellent suggestions as we worked together getting the manuscript to the publishing stage.

Mat Poirier, Boson, MA - thank you for coming to my aid on such short notice and producing the wonderful illustrations depicting the contents of this book including the cover.

Copyright Red Mountain Postcards.com – Images of Tunica, MS

Photo Image – Big Ben & London Bus by Pawel Libera, www.liberadesign.co.uk

Photo ©C.P.S.C. Scanavision - Niagara Falls-An aerial view of the Horseshoe Falls, ©Royal Specialty Sales, Toronto, ON

Special thanks to Lorraine Robazza, Chairperson, and June Ward, Manager, the Hockey Heritage North Museum, Kirkland Lake, ON, for clarifying information on the Kirkland Lake gold mining history and the famous NHL players who hailed from Kirkland Lake.

Thank you to Elizabeth Szucsik, Photo Lab Manager at Walmart's, Centennial Drive, Hamilton, ON; she was very helpful with the collage/photo images created for inclusion in this book.

Thanks to all the people interviewed who took time from their busy schedules to complete the interview forms and then met to polish their stories. May I take this opportunity to wish you success in your chosen careers and good health and fortune in all future endeavors.

To friends Marnie, Gail, Barbara, Peggy, June, Vickie, Judy, Linda, Sheila and others who had to listen to my concerns, frustrations and roadblocks while writing this book (Lee and Vivian too) – you are true friends and for that I am grateful.

To my husband, Len, 82 years old and still 'motoring' – you are my rock and have always been my Knight in Shining Armor. Your patience and understanding while writing this book will never be forgotten. We have been married going on 48 years and our marriage has probably survived this long because of the little trips, junkets and travel experiences with him/without him (he needs space).

To my dear daughter Kelly and son-in-law Steve - thanks for all your support; it is so appreciated. Carter and Erika – As Erika, my 11-year old granddaughter said "My Grammie is not a-knittin- sittin Grandma." My wish for you both, when you are older - visit and enjoy the Casinos as an occasional outing, but please respect this form of entertainment and I pray that you do not become addicted.

To Marnie - Thanks for the suggestion and help with the title of this book – it says it all; a big thanks for the proofing and editing as well.

Throughout this book, I have noted family, friends, and acquaintances that are now deceased. The game of life is the biggest game of all and life is shorter for some than others. One never knows when their 'game' is up. Enjoy what you can when you can.

As stated in the Introduction, I believe that gambling has become the "hidden sport" of many people world-wide, but the millions participating do not really want to acknowledge that they engage in this type of sport. Like any sport, you can get hurt while participating. If you gamble, admit it, don't be ashamed or get hurt financially. Respect this form of entertainment and enjoy it. If it stops being fun, it is time to leave. If you need help – get it!

## YOU CAN'T CHANGE WHAT YOU DON'T ACKNOWLEDGE
– Dr. Phil

It's not over 'til the fat lady sings – I cannot sing and it definitely isn't over!

Don't Sweat the Small Stuff; Life is Good and God Bless!

Commitment: A portion of the profits made from the sale of this book, after all expenses, will be donated to the Hamilton Alzheimer's Society.

Joan C.

# About the Author

Joan Campell (Surtees) was born in Kirkland Lake, ON in 1938. She graduated from K.L.C.V.I. and then moved to Hamilton, ON where she worked for Procter & Gamble for 7-1/2 years. She then moved to Ottawa and worked with the Federal Government in the Dept. of External Affairs. In 1964 she returned to Hamilton where she married husband Len (47 years). She worked for IBM before beginning a teaching career in the secondary system with the Hamilton Board of Education for 8 years, and then taught Office Administration, in the business department, Mohawk College A.A.&T. for 25 years. After retiring in 1998 from a 33-year teaching career, Joan now writes for Pearson Education Canada, Inc. She is currently working on the 8th ed. of the Pitman Office Handbook. This 600-pg. handbook is used in Business Programs in Community Colleges, Business Schools, Business and Government. Joan's education was with McMaster University, Hamilton, Ontario College of Teachers, Toronto, and Confederation College, Thunder Bay. She decided to write a book on gambling based on the interesting people she met, the casinos visited in Canada, the U.S. and other countries, and encouragement from family and friends.